The
Christian
Manager

A Call to Ministry

Shane P. Linder

Table Of Contents

About The Author

Shane Linder earned a Bachelor of Science Degree in Construction Management from Minnesota State University, Mankato after serving in the US Army Engineer Regiment in Panama. He has worked in Deep South Texas as a project manager in commercial building construction for over 17 years . He has managed multiple projects valued up to $13 million, overseeing over 100 employees on a given day. His experience includes cost estimating, expediting material deliveries, managing human resources, negotiating contracts, quality control, safety inspections, accounting and processing insurance claims.

Shane has served in his religious denomination as a church elder, deacon and several other lay positions. He has volunteered as a construction missionary in the US, El Salvador and Mexico. He is bilingual speaking both English and Spanish. He is also the author of the book Peculiar Christianity.

Introduction

"The fear of the Lord is the beginning of knowledge: but fools despise wisdom and instruction." Proverbs 1:7. Most people divide their lives into three areas: work, family and church. Yet God commands the Christian to bring glory to Him in all they do. Faith should over-shadow the family life and that of the profession. That is not to suggest one needs to "wear their faith on their sleeve" but rather that believers are to act like Christians even when outside of the church sanctuary.

This book is not about making money. There are many other books on the market about that. For ages many professing Christians have believed rich men cannot enter into the kingdom of heaven. Christ did not teach such. Christ taught that with God all things are possible. God does bless men and women in business. They earn their success honestly and give God the credit. While the world is filled with dishonesty in business, the Christian manager is like the beacon shining from a lighthouse. Many will despise them because their light reveals what is taking place in darkness. Others will be drawn into the light and have eternity to thank them.

Some believe in order to serve God in the ministry one must become a member of the clergy. One of the main purposes of this book is to show how management is itself a ministry. Those called to be managers ought not to take the calling lightly. A Christian will strive to win souls in every area of life: work, family and church.

"The Lord made Daniel and Joseph shrewd managers. He could work through them because they did not live to please their own inclination but to please God.

"The case of Daniel has a lesson for us. It reveals the fact that a businessman is not necessarily a sharp policy man. God can instruct him at every step. Daniel, while Prime Minister of the kingdom of Babylon, was a prophet of God, receiving the light of heavenly inspiration. Worldly, ambitious statesmen are represented in the word of God as the grass that grows up and as the flower of the grass that fadeth. Yet the Lord desires to have in His service intelligent men, men qualified for various lines of work. There is need of businessmen who will weave the grand principles of truth into all their transactions. And their talents should be perfected by most thorough study and training… Of Daniel we learn that all his business transactions, when subjected to the closest scrutiny, not one fault or error could be found. He was a sample of what every businessman may be. His history shows what may be accomplished by one who consecrates the strength of brain and bone and muscle, of heart and life, to the service of God." (P351 Christ Object Lessons)

There are many types of managers in the world. Managers are found in all sorts of businesses and every area of our society. The impact they have is incredible. It is no wonder God calls men and women to His[1] service in this ministry.

---

[1] In this volume pronouns in reference to God are capitalized to show respect for Him.

1

The Role Of Management

Management is defined as the persons controlling and directing a business or institution. The responsibility of management is therefore exactly that. A manager must be concerned about the interests of his or her company. If the manager is not who will be? While it is true the owner or stockholders are concerned about the company, they cannot do what those in management positions can. The reason a management team is put together is because the president of the company cannot do everything.

Let's take a moment to think about this concept. If a man knows how to fix cars he can open a mechanic shop. Yet being only one man he can only fix so many cars. If he wants to increase his earnings he needs to fix more cars. So he hires another mechanic. Soon he hires a team of mechanics. Yet he still wants to increase his earnings. So he opens another mechanic shop. Soon he has various mechanic shops so he hires shop managers because he cannot manage them all. It then becomes the managers' responsibility and obligation to look out for the interests of the company. The owner simply cannot do it all.

In the twenty-fifth chapter of Matthew we find the parable of the talents. Starting in verse 14 there was a man who was to travel to a foreign land so he assembled a management team. To each "manager" he gave a number of talents according to his ability. While he was gone two of these managers invested the money while one hid his money in the ground. When the owner returned the two managers who had invested the money returned to the owner the money and it earnings. Both of these two managers received thanks and promotion. The one who hid his money returned it to the owner. He claimed he hid it because he was afraid of the owner and didn't want to lose any of it. The owner was upset that the manager had done nothing with it. That manager got fired.

Besides the spiritual lessons we can draw from the metaphors employed, in a literal sense, this parable teaches us that managers need to accept challenges of responsibility. When responsibility is placed upon a manager he or she ought to do what is in the best interest of the company. The manager's first concern shouldn't be how this responsibility will make him or her look. That was the manager's problem in the parable. He was afraid of his boss. He was putting his personal interests in front of the interests of his boss. Good managers must not put personal interests first.

Look at this parable again and ask yourself, "If management doesn't look out for the company who will?" The owner makes the point in the parable that the buried money could have a least been placed in a bank account and earned interest. Because the bad manager did not look out for the owner's interests, no one did. The owner's point is that a banker would have profited him more than did this manager. That manager's job was the same as all managers. Managers are to look out for their companies.

Christian Priorities

Why should the manager give that type of dedication to his or her company? What has the company done to deserve someone looking out for its interests? First we must ask, "What is a company"? Is a company buildings and equipment? Is a company registered documents with the state? Is a company its employees? Is a company all of these things? There are companies Christians will not want to manage. What Christian would want to manage an abortion clinic? What Christian would want to manage a company that cheats and deceives its clients? If a manager cannot justify looking out for the company's interest he or she shouldn't be working for the company.

Successful companies are what drive the economy. They compensate their employees so they can provide for their needs. When a company is successful it can grow, adding more jobs. It can promote employees. It can train more workers. These employees then use their wages to provide for themselves and families. In so doing they stimulate the economy more. A country with a booming economy will provide more opportunities for more people. The key to an advancing economy is creating good-paying jobs and education. Successful companies can do both of those. As Christians we want to be part of a successful company.

The author is a project manager and estimator for a commercial construction firm in Texas. He has worked in that position for over seventeen years. The job can be very stressful. Many people he works with are not Christians. He works with people who want to cheat his company out every penny they can. Others are two-faced people who will talk nice and try to charm him so they can later cut corners on one of the projects. He works with architects that often try to make his firm pay for the mistakes they made in the plans. Some clients try to get him to do extras at no additional cost. He supervises employees that often are not looking out for the company's interests. He understands the reality that we can work in the world and yet not be of the world.

As manager our first commitment is to God. We must not do anything as a manager that will jeopardize our relationship with Him. Often times we need to make quick, silent prayers throughout the day asking for divine guidance. Some may view such behavior as fanatical. It isn't. Without Christ we are selfish. A man cannot be half the manager without Christ as he can be with Him. One needn't make prayers public. To do so may well be counter-productive. Prayers are often a private matter between God and the believer. One can simply ask to handle a situation as Christ would handle it. Pretty much like WWJD.

A manager's second commitment is to his or her family. Being a manager can be hard on a marriage and a family. If the job should ever interfere with the marriage, there should be no reservation about professional Christian counseling or changing jobs if necessary. A man vows to love his wife in sickness and health, richer or poorer, until death do us part. That type of a commitment is never made to a company. Sometimes overtime is required and work needs to be taken home. There is no rule that can be established regarding this. Circumstances determine how much overtime is too much and how much office work can be brought home.

The author has been known to take work home on the weekend and work late at times. Often times a manager will work through the lunch hour to try to keep up.

A manager's third commitment is to his or her country. Nothing done should harm one's country. This means obeying laws, codes and doing nothing that would knowingly do harm to the community.

The manager's fourth commitment is to the company. The money that makes the house payment and puts food on the table comes from the company. That isn't to say the salary isn't earned. Of course it is. It is a simply stating a fact. The earnings come from the company. One could say the salary is a result of the manager's education and hence he or she should contribute to his or her university's alumni fund. Yet they paid all their tuition and dues when they went to school. How could they still owe them something? Although the salary is earned and the schooling was paid for, there is an unspoken debt of gratitude one should have toward both their company and university. Should an animal bite the hands that feed it and say, "There are other hands not far away that will feed me too"? Of course not. Should a manager than do less than his or her 100% and say, "No big deal I can get another job in less than two weeks"? Of course not. We ought to have a commitment to the firm that pays us for our talents.

Humility In Management

The manager that thinks of him or herself as a big shot and those under him or her as little guys is in error. Galations 6:3 speaks to this. "For if a man think himself to be something, when he is nothing, he deceiveth himself". Apart from Christ each of us are "nothing". Christ made this clear in John 15:5. He said, "without Me ye can do nothing." Christ is our model, our example. Matthew 18:11 states, "For the Son of man is come to save that which was lost." Christ came here for the betterment of man. John 1:1 and 14 says, "In the beginning was the Word, and the Word was with God, and the Word was God... And the Word was made flesh and dwelt among us". Christ was the biggest big shot of all big shots yet He came here for the betterment of humanity. How does this example relate to a manager's attitude about him or herself?

"The fear of the Lord is to hate evil: pride, and arrogancy, and the evil way, and the froward mouth, do I hate. Counsel is mine, and sound wisdom: I am understanding; I have strength. By Me kings reign, and princes decree justice. By Me princes rule, and nobles, even all the judges of the earth." Prov. 8:13-16. God desires Christian managers to be humble and reflect Him. Christ's example should not be made light of. It does a Christina manager good to meditate on the humbleness of Christ's life on this Earth. He who dwelled in a city of mansions with golden streets, had no home to call His own. It was not only His lack of material wealth that made Jesus humble. The way He related to the simplest of people was only as a humble man would.

Bernie Anderson tells the story of the arrogant donkey that one day returned to the stable boasting of his eventful day. He told all of his animal friends how when he entered into Jerusalem there were crowds of people greeting him saying hosanna in the highest, blessed be the king and they were all waiving palm branches and bowing down to him. Why he even picked up a hitchhiker but that didn't seem to dampen anyone's spirits. The donkey wasn't only arrogant but foolish. The donkey's only glory could be found in Christ who rode in it. The same is true for each businessman and woman. It is by Christ that kings and princes rule. Christ enables politicians, businessmen, actors and teachers as well as blue-collar workers to achieve their status in this world *even if they don't believe it.* "Remember the Lord thy God, for it is He that giveth thee the power to get wealth" (Deut. 8:18) God sends the rain to fall on both the good and the bad. The words of Christ must be part of our daily life. "Without Me ye can do nothing."

In looking out for a company managers must have the betterment of those in their charge in mind. Those who work under them are a major part of their success or failure. Some managers are concerned about those under them out shining them. Some managers work to prevent the betterment of those under them. Such a course is not in the best interest of one's company and is motivated by selfishness and fear. A manager should work to develop and encourage growth in those under him or her. A good manager uses Christ as the Example and does not let pride or fear be part of the picture.

Humility is such an important ingredient in Christian management. Being humble does not mean letting people take advantage of the manager or the company. It means understanding that the manager, is only one part of something big. Paul outlined this concept so well in First Corinthians chapter 12. All parts of the body are to be valued. The head needs the feet and the eye needs the hand. Think back to the mechanic who has a number of mechanic shops with various shop managers. Each shop manager and each mechanic is part of his success. Humility will teach him that he is to value his mechanics like the head values the feet. Is one position in the company more important than another? If the company only had a president who would fix the cars? The president would then be the mechanic again.

Some disagree with such reasoning and ask, "If the president's position is equal to the mechanics' position, why does the president make more money?" Is an apple more valuable than an avocado? Why is an avocado worth more money? Part of the answer is supply and demand. There are more mechanics than presidents. That is not the entire answer. The president also has more responsibility and more risk. Those are the two biggest factors. The mechanic is only responsible for the cars he or she works on. The president is responsible for all the cars all his or her mechanics work on. The most the mechanic can lose is his or her job. The president can lose the company. The president is able to generate more revenue than the mechanic. The mechanic generates revenue by repairing cars brought into the shop. The president generates revenue by opening new shops, purchasing more efficient equipment, training, marketing, and purchasing auto parts and supplies. The amount of revenue one mechanic can make for the company is limited by the amount of work that can be produced. The amount of revenue the president can make in one day could be greater than the mechanic's annual salary. Yet the fact that one position deserves a higher salary does not mean that the person holding that position is of greater value.

A Christian manager will not speak down to an employee. It has been said that a job does not bring honor to a man rather it is the man that brings honor to a job. There are many honorable janitors while there are many dishonorable managers. The Christian manager will treat the employee as part of the company's success. When the employee needs correction the manager will correct the employee just as God corrects us. Christ says in Revelation 3:19, "As many as I love, I rebuke and chasten" and so the Christian manager will be with his or her erring employees. Such correction does not elevate the manager above the employee in a sense of value. The Christian manager will do well to pray for guidance regarding the administration of correction.

A People Business

Most forms of management are about people. While managing a business involves balancing books, chasing the accounts payable and keeping track of inventory, managing people is part of most every manager's job description. While the author is in the construction business, that business is about people. It is about getting people to do what they need to do, how they need to do it and when it needs to be done. This holds true regardless if the company administers medical treatment or packages kitty litter.

Working with people starts with the company's employees. Every manager wants employees that want the company to be successful. An Army platoon sergeant had a flier on his wall that said, "Your men won't care how much you know until they know how much you care." Workers can become very endeared to their managers. The author worked for some great managers in a couple of restaurants while in college. They treated him well and he performed his best for them. Employees often will work hard, miss less work and have a better attitude when there is mutual respect between worker and manager.

The opposite is also true. Some employees do not perform well because of management. Such employees are sometimes discharged only to go on and become outstanding employees for the next company. Most of the difference is management. A manager's lack of people skills can result in poor performance in the workers. While in High School the author was told by a friend of how he and some of his coworkers stole a number of rolls of felt-paper from their boss while roofing one summer. They had nothing to gain in so doing. They had no use for the felt-paper and knew no one who wanted to buy it. They stole it out of spite for their boss. His lack of people skills cost him in inventory.

A good manager will want to manage his or her employees in such a way that they want to perform well. It should be the goal of the Christian manager that the employees perform well not due to someone looking over their shoulder rather because it brings joy and satisfaction to do a good job. This is the type of service Christ desires from us. We serve Him not because He is looking over our shoulder but rather because we love Him and desire to please Him. A truly successful manager will have employees that respond likely.

During a booming economy, businessmen cannot coldly place demands on their workers without any praise or incentive. Employees in the work force will not stay with a firm where they do not feel needed or are not treated well. There are many companies willing to treat employees good with ads in newspapers, employment offices and on the Internet. A manager that lacks human relationship skills will cost his or her company a great deal by increasing turnover among its employees.

The Great Recession caused a change in attitude among many businessmen and women. Twenty five years of prosperity had created a labor market that favored skilled workers. As unemployment rose and the mass media stirred up a national environment of fear, many businesses, both large and small, took advantage of the situation. Many companies cut wages and required salaried employees to work longer hours. Many cut benefits such as paid holidays and retirement plan contributions. In many cases these changes were made without any financial justification. The businesses making the cuts were still bringing in the target profit margins. A construction company, for example, that had bid a project with a specified amount of money for payroll, cut payroll even though they still collected the money for labor that they included in their bid.

Workers grow accustomed to living on the amount of money they make. A business cannot take something back without some sort of consequences. When a company gives an employee a raise, some sort of benefit or perks and later takes it back there will be consequences. When a company tries to do that, what happens is that they lose their best and brightest or the most hardworking and efficient workers. The slackers, the ones that don't work hard and really are just lucky to have a job, are the ones that will stick with a company even when the company lowers their wages and takes away benefits. The workers that actually produce for the company will be enticed to leave. It is just a matter of time. Another company will compensate them what they were making. It might happen right away or it may not happen until the economic cycle turns up. One thing is for sure. If a company cuts wages or benefits, the employees are not likely to feel any sense of loyalty or commitment to the firm.

There is a certain psychological mind-set that causes a company to cut wages and benefits. An economic downturn is filled with companies failing. A panic grips company owners as they are only humans and subject to their own emotions. So they quickly look at ways they can cut costs and thus strengthen their company's ability to weather the storm. Payroll is one of the biggest costs for many companies so it is often the first and easiest to start cutting. However there is a train of thought that says it is far better to lay-off workers that are not needed than it is to reduce the wages or benefits of those that stay with the company. When a company reduces wages and benefits they send a message to the workers and it isn't one that increases loyalty, efficiency or moral. It should be the last thing a company does and only done when absolutely necessary to keep the company afloat. In the event that it is done, when the economy allows the company to prosper again, something needs to be done to win back the confidence of those whose compensation was reduced.

Christian managers should take time to understand employees as people. This involves evaluating their personality and behavior style. Many managers get too wrapped up in their specific industry and lose sight of the human element. Not everyone has the same behavior style. Knowing the behavior styles of one's employees will direct one how to communicate and treat that person. This will allow an increase in productivity. Employees with certain behavior styles are more efficient doing certain tasks than others. It behooves a manager to take the time to evaluate employees and place them in the most appropriate position.

Understanding personality types will go a long way in effectively communicating with others. A big part of a manager's job is communicating. While a manager may be very ambitious and highly intelligent he or she will not fulfill their potential if they cannot communicate well with others. One major communication barrier is personality. If a manager is unwilling to be flexible he or she may find it quite difficult to communicate with some personalities. It is often futile to expect an employee to change their personality type to that which compliments the manager. When a manager understands the employee's personality type it is the manager who can change his or her means of communication.

There are some that want to dismiss all these personality characterization tests as having little merit. Part of it is that it is easy to want to avoid being labeled into a category. However a person of one personality type can change into another type. In fact the more one walks with Christ the more they become like Him. They start to have more of the character assets of all the personality types and less character liabilities of any of them. This small volume cannot go into the various personality types. The author is not an expert in the field. Books and seminars are available on this topic. Understanding why peers and subordinates do and think as they do will enables managers to communicate with them better.

A manager will work with all types of people. As a manager, and as a Christian, we are given the opportunity that many others will never have to influence those we work with. Some think too highly of themselves and need to be taught humility. Others think too lowly of themselves and need to know they have value. Some struggle with resentment and need patience. Hours, weeks, months and sometimes years are spent with employees. This time is a God-given opportunity for Christian managers to let others see Him in us.

Christian managers can influence an employee toward our loving Savior. While some companies do not allow proselytizing during company hours, our actions are in most cases more important than our words. Telling others about Jesus when they have not asked about Him, can backfire. It can cause others to view the Christian manager as "holier-than-thou" and start magnifying the character defects the Christian has not yet overcome. In many cases the example is what others need to see. Verbalizing the Christian faith is most effective when those working with the Christian manager actually ask about the faith. The Christian manager can show employees our Savior even if speaking of Him is not allowed.

Many employees have never worked with someone who is interested in them as a person. Of course the manager must be interested in the company. Yet we do not need to decide if we should be more interested in our company or its employees. In the book *The Art of Managing People* it is stated well, "We can be more effective managers by increasing both our understanding of others and our skills for communicating effectively in order to build more productive interpersonal relationships with employees. By becoming more interpersonally effective, we can make our employees and the organization more effective. *Everybody can win!*" (p.16)

Responsibility

Chasing money is another responsibility that many managers must do. There have been many companies that have gone out of business because they did not keep after their accounts payable. The Lord said, "The laborer is worthy of his hire." This has been used often to justify compensating employees for their work with livable wages. In the same respect a company should be compensated for the goods and services provided by it. In most cases, the longer accounts payable are left unpaid the less likely they will ever be paid. The Christian manager should not feel guilty about making others pay their bills - not unless they were sold a product or service by questionable means. Don't misunderstand this point to say exceptions and mercy should never be given. Exceptions are exceptions because they are not part of the ordinary. The ordinary for some businesses is to let accounts payable almost take care of themselves. Such action is to neglect the company.

Managers are not only to feel a sense of responsibility to their company but also to God. Many managers think of themselves as working for a specific company or person. While that is true in a very real sense, there is more than just that. Deuteronomy 10:14 says, "the heaven of heavens is the Lord's thy God, the earth also, with all that therein is." It is with such a thought that the hyminist wrote, "We give Thee but Thine own, whatever the gift may be, All that we have is Thine alone, a trust, O Lord from Thee."

Those who own companies are but trusted servants. It doesn't matter if they are trustworthy or not. They have in their possession, and perhaps control, assets that belong to God. Therefore we are all working for God. God is the ultimate Owner of every corporation and firm. Consider it for a moment. Who is the owner of all the beds in a hospital? Of the jets of an airline? Of the desks in a law office? Job learned this lesson prior to losing his possessions. "Naked came I out of my mother's womb, and naked shall I return thither: the Lord gave, and the Lord hath taken away; blessed be the name of the Lord."

Being a manager should be a joy. The work of a manager should bring one into a closer walk with the Lord. A manager's work should not be one that causes loss of sleep, endless irritation, heart attack or stroke. The Christian faith should follow the loyal and faithful manager out of the church and into the home and office. Yet many managers are plagued with anxiety. They do not know how to leave their work at the office. They do lose sleep and worry. Struggling with anxiety is difficult and there is no easy solution. Yet there is a way to reduce anxiety over a period of time by increasing faith. One must trust in God. Not trust that God will always cause things to turn out the way we want them but that He is looking out for us in ways we may not always see. "And we know that all things work together for good to them that love God" (Romans 8:28). Goals and ambitions must be surrendered to the will of God.

Laurie Beth Jones wrote in *Jesus Inc.*, "If sin is separation from God, what could be more sin-full than choosing to devote your life energies and talents to work that does not honor God? If your work does not honor God, it does not honor you. And conversely if it does not honor you, it does not honor God." We needn't preach to others verbally to honor God. Conducting ourselves as godly men and women brings honor to Him. Doing business under His direction brings honor to Him. How one can honor God as a manager is the theme of this book.

In this book there is a chapter on continual improvement. This involves taking inventory of ourselves. Every good manager wants his or her investments to appreciate. The manager's work habits, abilities and knowledge are the investment he or she can most control. It then behooves each manager to be painfully honest when evaluating what he or she lacks and what needs to be done to improve.

A chapter on planning has also been included in this small volume. Planning is often a manager's key to accomplishing what needs to be done. Many managers that lack planning skills must make up for them with endless excuses. A manager with well-developed planning skills can be a great witness for what Christ can accomplish. Christ was not conceived in Mary on the spur of the moment. The plan of salvation was decided upon by the Godhead long before the fall in the garden. As we study Christ's ministry we see He did not run it impulsively, rather He thought ahead.

The chapter after planning is about customer service. Customers are responsible for a business' income. Most managers realize that yet many of the employees working under them do not. Customer service involves training and leading by example. The Christian manager should always treat the customer respectfully and humor him or her when required. Those that work for the government may not be concerned about customer service due to lack of competition. The Christian manager ought always to treat the customer the same.

The final chapters are about problem solving and profits. What defines a manager in this regard? What defines a problem or its solution? The Christian manager will not allow either pride or blame interfere with facing and solving problems as they arise. The Christian will be distinguished by his or her manner of handling stressful situations as they arise. There is no problem to which God does not have the answer. The Christian manager will know how to seek that answer and how to utilize it.

A Christian manager strives to do his or her job in such a way to bring glory to God. Dishonesty larks around each corner. Complacency desires a home and impatience pleads for position. A close walk with Christ will cause these temptations to fade and the work of a manager to become very rewarding. Christ taught us to keep our spiritual priorities ahead of our material priorities. "But seek ye first the kingdom of God, and His righteousness; and all these things shall be added unto you." Laurie Beth Jones stated it well in *Jesus, Inc.* "Spiritreneurs do not set out to harness God in order to make more money. Rather, spiritreneurs allow God to harness them, and in so doing experience glory."

2

Continual Improvement

Too many managers become complacent in their job. They start to act like they have nothing more to learn or if they do it is not much. Most are willing to admit the need to learn new technology but not much more outside of that. The learning curve becomes quite flat for all too many. While the learning curve will always start off quite sharp when any manager starts a new job or takes a new position it does not have to level off as much as it normally does.

There are several reasons why the learning curve levels off. Continual improvement is more possible than many believe. It does not come easy. It requires continual effort. It requires self-examination and willingness to accept criticism. Managers are not born; they are made. The making of a manager can be a continuous process.

As sinners we must always beware of self. Self always wants to justify itself. When in error, self despises being revealed as it is. We must put our interests outside of self. That is why priorities are important: God, Family, Country, and Company. These four things must come before self. The Bible often refers to self as the heart. This is the case with Jeremiah 17:9. Here the Hebrew word leb is translated as heart. Stong's Concordance defines leb as, "the will or even the intellect". The verse says, "The heart is deceitful above all things, and desperately wicked: who can know it?"

It is a valid question. If the human will and intellect is deceitful above all things and desperately wicked, who can know it? The answer we find in Psalms 139:23, 24. Only God can know it. Remember the story of when Christ asked Peter who he thought He was? Peter responded, "Thou art the Christ, the Son of the living God. And Jesus answered and said unto him, 'Blessed art thou, Simon Barjona: for flesh and blood hath not revealed it unto thee, but my Father which is in heaven.'" It was not Peter's intellect that figured out Jesus was the Christ. Peter's intellect was deceitful and wicked. It was the Holy Spirit that revealed to Peter that Jesus was the Christ.

This theme runs throughout the Scripture. We must not trust in ourselves. This is made abundantly clear in Isaiah 56: 8, 9. "For my thoughts are not your thoughts, neither are your ways my ways, saith the Lord. For as the heavens are higher than the earth, so are my ways higher than your ways, and my thoughts than your thoughts." In light of this, Paul's statement in Galations 6:3 is quite simple, "For if a man think himself to be something, when he is nothing, he deceiveth himself."

There are two ways to acquire wealth - with God's help or without it. That is not to say there are no ethical, honest businessmen or women who are not Christian or of another religion. Most Christians are familiar with the passage of Matthew 19:24, "It is easier for a camel to go through the eye of a needle, than for a rich man to enter into the kingdom of God." However we are also familiar with verse 26, "with God all things are possible."

There are several examples of rich, godly men in the Bible. Abraham, Jacob, Joseph, Job, David, Solomon, the centurion of great faith and Nicodemus are some. Ellen White wrote in *The Desire of Ages*, "To the rich, God has given wealth that they may relieve and comfort His suffering children." (P.639) We are valuable to God and He wants to use us. We need not be full-time preachers to be used by God. 1 Corinthians 12:28 lists governments or administrations as a spiritual gift. As businessmen and women we can testify of our God and use His blessings to honor Him.

That is not to suggest that Christian business people ought to wear their faith on their sleeve, so to speak, and advertise their Christianity. Some businesses that broadcast their Christian faith have been known as being scoundrels and reflected poorly on the faith. Rather than broadcasting our Christianity by print or verbal means, it behooves the Christian to testify with his or her behavior – act like a Christian. Let people know something is different by the way we interact with others and conduct ourselves. We shouldn't be ashamed to admit to one's faith but we don't need to trumpet it either.

We can only be successful Christian businessmen and women when we recognize we are desperately in need of divine guidance. Such divine guidance requires continuous improvement. Psalms 119:105 says, "Thy word is a lamp unto my feet, and a light unto my path:" This tells us life is like a journey on a path. A lamp is required because the Christian is to be always advancing on the journey. The lamp required is the Word of God.

This is not to discourage any managers that feel they may be being called into another line of work to ignore the calling. Although a person may have one spiritual gift, God can still give them another. A manager may receive the calling to leave business to be a pastor, a teacher, a doctor or an evangelist. Likewise those with other spiritual gifts may be called upon to go to another area of ministry. The point being made is that managers are in a ministry. The work done may not be as elevated as the work of a pastor or doctor yet lives are still influenced. The manager's example is a testimony to employees and associates.

We must understand there is a connection between our professional lives and our spiritual lives. Each affects the other. As we grow in Christ we become a better employee and/or employer. 1 Corinthians 10:31 tells us, "whatsoever ye do, do all to the glory of God." Our spiritual lives affect every aspect of us. Review the experience of Jacob with Laban in Genesis 30:27. God blessed Jacob's labor and this blessing resulted in making Laban a richer man. For that reason Laban did not want Jacob to quit working for him. God is still the same today. As we grow closer to Christ He will bless our work.

Many find that as their careers have progressed not everything they have learned has been for their benefit. There are bad habits and shortcuts that are started that they did not know about at the beginning. Our twelve-step friends in self-improvement groups teach their members to take a regular personal inventory. A personal inventory is an inventory of one's character assets and liabilities. This is done so the assets may be improved while the liabilities may be eliminated. King David asked for God's help in doing this task. In Psalms 139: 23, 24 he

13

wrote, "Search me O God, and know my heart: try me, and know my thoughts: and see if there be any wicked way in me, and lead me in the way everlasting."

Here is a sample management evaluation a manager can use to prioritize efforts for improvements.

Manager Evaluation		
	Importance To My Job (1-5)	Amount I need To Improve (1-5)
1 Technical knowledge of my industry		
2 Constructive discipline of employees		
3 Constructive praise of employees		
4 Ability to accept criticism		
5 Letter writing skills		
6 Conversational skills		
7 Ability to use authority		
8 Time management skills		
9 Computer skills		
10 Record keeping skills		
11 Problem solving skills		
12 Ability to access needed information		
13 Ability to efficiently run a meeting		
14 Ability to motivate others		
15 Listening skills		
16 Note taking skills		
17 Ability to help others		
18 Physical appearance (hygiene, dress, etc.)		
19 Vocabulary skills		
20 Non-verbal skills		
21 Proper sleep at night		
22 Legal knowledge of my industry		
23 Attitude		
24 Ability to keep up with paperwork		
25 Ability to prioritize		

Technical Knowledge

Too many managers do not spend enough, if any, time reading literature about their industry. Many believe once they earn their diploma there is no longer a need to study. Mark Eppler says in his book *Management Mess-Ups*, "Studies indicate that reading is a lost art for the majority of college graduates, with more than 70 percent of them never reading another book in their area of expertise." It is no wonder the learning curve levels off.

The first item on the inventory is technical knowledge. Experience is bound to increase this but it's not the only thing that can. Paying attention to what is going on can often make experience more valuable. There are seminars, conferences and a world of literature available to managers as a means of continuing education. Literature ranges from brochures and magazines to books and newspapers. Too many claim they haven't enough time for such things. Yet if they examine how much time they waste in needless activities they will become very aware of missed opportunities to learn.

Constructive Discipline of Employees

Constructive discipline of employees is not about wagging the finger and assigning blame. Too many managers enjoy insulting their employees and think of it as constructive criticism. It is all too easy to become hypocrites in so doing. Constructive criticism has one objective: to increase the value of the employee being criticized. Insulting does not build rather it breaks down. Insults do not solve problems, rather they create new ones.

Mark Eppler stated it well, "Resisting the chance to prove someone wrong can be difficult. It takes a great deal of maturity, not to mention foresight, to avoid blame and press on to solving the problem." (ibid. p.127) The wisdom of Solomon tells us, "To everything there is a season, and a time to every purpose under heaven... a time to keep silence, and a time to speak." The idea that maturity and foresight are required before giving constructive criticism is thought provoking.

Learning to offer constructive criticism is important. Hypocrisy needs to be avoided if criticism is going to have much merit. Our peers and employees will judge us on our examples. When offering constructive criticism one needs to bear in mind that often times one way isn't always the only way. One doesn't want to discourage creativity. Remember the story about the disciples returning from their first missionary trip? John reported, "Master, we saw one casting out devils in Thy name; and forbade him, because he followeth not us." What does that sound like? It sounds a lot like "My way is the only way". Christ replied, "Forbid him not: for he that is not against us is for us." There is more than one way to skin a cat.

Constructive Praise of Employees

How important is it to praise employees? Praise supplies motivation. Look at the example of our military. The military is filled with examples of praise and discipline. Praise also supplies satisfaction. Many prefer to work for a company that gives job satisfaction than a company that pays a higher salary. Workers with higher motivation and satisfaction are more likely to work more efficiently. When you praise a worker for something they do he or she is more likely to listen to your criticism later.

Ability to Accept Criticism

"Now no chastening for the present seemeth to be joyous, but grievous: nevertheless afterward it yeldeth the peaceable fruit of righteousness unto them which are exercised thereby." Hebrew 12:11. That is a mouthful. No criticism, no matter how constructive, is going to seem joyous although later it produces good results. The ability to accept criticism is really part of being humble. Those that struggle with pride are going to struggle more with accepting criticism. Jesus said, "As many as I love, I rebuke and chasten". Criticism shouldn't be greeted with resistance.

In the book *As Bill Sees It*, written by one of the co-founders of Alcoholics Anonymous, is a copy of a profound letter. It says, "Thanks much for your letter of criticism. I'm certain that had it not been for its strong critics, A.A. would have made slower progress. For myself, I have come to set a high value on the people who have criticized me, whether they have seemed reasonable critics or unreasonable ones. Both have restrained me from doing much worse than I actually have done. The unreasonable ones have taught me, I hope, a little patience. But the reasonable ones have always done a great job for all of A.A. - and have taught me many a valuable lesson." (p. 326) That sounds a lot like Psalms 141:5, "Let the righteous smite me; it shall be a kindness: and let him reprove me; it shall be an excellent oil, which shall not break my head".

Letter Writing Skills

Letter writing and conversational skills will be discussed in greater detail in the next chapter. Communication skills are important to all managers. If a manager is fortunate enough to have a secretary that can help in this area they ought to be treated *and paid* well or they are apt to find another employer that will accommodate them so.

Conversational Skills

A conversation is a verbal interaction between two or more people. In business there is small talk and shop talk. Small talk discusses issues unrelated to one's industry. Examples can be the weather, sports, family or even politics and religion although it is not always permitted or wise to discuss the last two in some work environments. Shop talk discusses issues related to the industry one is working in. Both of these typically have their place. Improved conversational skills comes with improved communication skills which includes listening as well as speaking.

Ability to Use Authority

To measure our ability to use authority is to measure how well we can get those we are in charge of to perform. It was noted of Christ, "He taught them as one that had authority". Christ's authority did not come from the tone of His voice. Christ had extensive knowledge, communication skills and was the perfect Example. He needs to be the Example of how to use authority. The ability to use authority will increase as a manager's knowledge, communication skills and the example does.

No one has all knowledge so each person ought to have an open mind. Yet a conscientious manager cannot let others influence decisions in their favor if it is not for the best of the firm. A manager often finds him or herself with 100 advisers when it comes to making some decisions. There are vendors, contractors and employees always telling them what decisions should be made. The manager must always consider what is best for the firm because often times an advisor's motives are dubious.

One of the reasons military experience looks so attractive on a resume is because those in the military are taught how to accept authority. Everyone in the military is under authority. This was a lesson Bill Clinton found out the hard way as Commander In Chief. The centurion of great faith understood what it meant to be under authority. He told Christ, "I am a man under authority, having soldiers under me; and I say to this man, Go and he goeth; and to another, Come, and he cometh; and to my servant, Do this, and he doeth it." (Matt: 8:9) The centurion understood being under authority is doing what you are told.

This is a lesson that is hard for many to learn. After Jesus calmed the sea, the disciples exclaimed, "What manner of Man is this, that even the wind and the sea obey Him?" They had not grasped the centurion's lesson on authority given just a short time before. Being under authority means being submissive. It means obeying. Look at the rewards it brings. It endears. Perhaps that is why Scripture says the centurion's servant "was dear unto him."

Scripture speaks clear on the issue of being under the authority of other men. "Let every soul be subject unto the higher powers. For there is no power but of God: the powers that be are ordained of God. Whosoever therefore resisteth the power, resisteth the ordinance of God: and they shall receive to themselves damnation." (Romans 13:1,2) The exception to this is when believers are told to do something that violates the law of God. Christ rebuked those that placed man's word above God's Word, "Full well ye reject the commandment of God, that ye may keep your own tradition." (Mark 7:9)

Those in the military are instructed not to follow orders that are against the Geneva Convention. All members are to question whether or not orders given are legal orders. God has given the same command to believers regarding the orders given by men. Believers are to question whether or not they violate His law. Managers do well not only to question if what they are told to do violates a law or regulation but additionally if it is in the best interest of the company. In respect to laws, rules and regulations, a manager's first obligation is to God, then civil authorities and then to one's company. Advice from advisors must always be considered in light of this.

The author recalls a story of a construction manager telling a superintendent working under him to proceed with a phase of construction. The superintendent did so without looking at the plans. In the end the work was not done correctly and had to be redone. The superintendent's response was to blame the manager by saying, "He told me to do it." Orders from a superior do not relieve one from the responsibility of looking out for the company's interests. While the construction manager was partially to blame, the superintendent neglected his responsibility to assure the plans are followed.

When a manager finds him or herself under the authority of an overbearing boss it may be time to send the resumes out. It is better to look for another job than to fight against authority. Many conflicts can be worked out and Christian managers should try to do so. Jesus taught, "Blessed are the peacemakers: for they shall be called the children of God." (Mat. 5:9) That being said, there are some hard-headed, overbearing people that are closed-minded and make everyone around them miserable. In such circumstances it is often best for the manger to dust off his or her shoes and move on.

Time Management Skills

Once time is spent it cannot be recovered. Time management skills give managers the ability to budget time. More can be done in each day with better time management. Much time management is discipline. Frivolous tasks and conversation can eat away a day by taking a few minutes here and a few minutes there. Then at the day's end one wonders why nothing much got accomplished. Another component of time management is planning. That will be discussed more in a later chapter. This is a skill that can increase our value to our employer and reduce some late office hours.

The urgent often takes priority over the important. Urgent tasks have a way demanding time and distracting a manager away from tasks that are more important. A phone call or an email can easily take a manager's attention off from an important task and shift it unto an urgent, but much less important task. One method to deal with these tasks is to assign each task a priority rating. Next to each task on a manager's "To Do" is a number indicating the tasks priority. While emails and phone calls may distract a manager for a moment, a quick review of the "To Do" list with priority-rated tasks can help keep him or her focused on the important.

Computer Skills

While computer skills are required in today's business world many managers are only learning what they need to get by. There are many missed opportunities to increase these skills. Educational opportunities abound for learning more computer skills. Computer workshops, night classes and online programs are offered by a variety of schools and businesses. A manager can be much more effective when he or she learns how to use all of the technology that a company invests in.

Companies have been known to purchase technology without providing the education to use it. This can be as simple as replacing Android phones with iPhones and not providing Apple training. Even if an iPhone can do more than its Android counterpart, in the hands of an untrained manager, it will be less useful and probably result in a lot of wasted time. The same holds true for other types of technology.

Record Keeping Skills

Good record keeping skills can make a manager's job easier and more efficient in more than one way. Depending upon the industry, records are kept differently. Some records are not kept due to laziness. This is something a Christian manager should work to prevent. Good records are used for future reference, planning, litigation and accountability. Record keeping does not happen by default. While some records may be more important than others, we need to honestly evaluate our efforts and abilities.

A company should have a filing system that all the managers use. This will allow a manager or an administrative assistant to find files in another manager's files. If each manager or assistant has their own way of filing things, in the absence of that person, information may be nearly impossible to find. Today many files are kept electronically and protected with passwords. This information should always be accessible by at least two people. One being the manager creating the files and the other an office administrator – either the owner, book-keeper or administrative assistant. In the event that a manager would quit, be terminated or die, someone else needs to be able to access the files quickly and easily.

Problem Solving Skills

Managers are problem solvers. A manager complaining about things not going right does not understand the nature of the job. It is easy to say that if only everything and everyone did things right there would be no problems. In a sinful world, neither everything nor everyone is ever going to be just right. Remember the example of the mechanic who bought a number of mechanic shops? The reason he hires shop managers is not only to supervise the mechanics but to solve problems that come up.

When a problem comes up it is not the time to assign blame. Too many mangers look to find fault. That is an emotional response, not a reason-based one. When confronted with a problem many managers react by looking to blame someone for the problem. Blame does not create solutions. Revelation 12:19 says Satan is the "accuser of our brethren". As problem solvers, managers need to first seek a solution. After the problem has been dealt with constructive criticism may be given. More on this theme will be discussed in a later chapter.

Ability to Access Needed Information

A manager's ability to access needed information will make him or her of much greater value. A manager may realize the need for a better filing system when unable to find proposals or letters when required with little notice. If a manager is determined to continually improve this is an area that needs to be evaluated. Accessing information is not just about a good filing system. This includes knowledgeable use of industry reference books, textbooks, periodicals, the Internet and contacts.

A manager's contacts can be great source of needed information. Company gray-hairs often have experience and perspectives that younger managers do not. A good manager will work to put together a network of contacts that he or she can draw upon. Proverbs 11:13 says, "in the multitude of counselors there is safety".

Ability to Efficiently Run a Meeting

One of the biggest wastes of time in a manager's day frequently are meetings and the current trend seems to be increasing the number of them in some industries. A Christian manager will not want to waste time any more than money. A good meeting has a specified purpose and agenda. The meeting is run by one individual who keeps it on track. Minutes are kept and made available soon after the meeting. Books and seminars are available to managers wanting to improve their ability to run an effective meeting.

Meetings are often used to put people on the hot seat and pressure them into making decisions or prioritizing a task. A manager can anticipate getting put on the hot seat and should thus prepare for it. Sometimes it is useful to rehearse a meeting before with a co-worker. When a manager goes into a meeting unprepared, it can be disastrous. An unprepared manager can lose an account or destroy a company's reputation in a meeting.

Ability to Motivate Employees

A good manager needs to be able to motivate employees and peers. There are two trains of thought in management. The first assumes employees are basically lazy and work because life requires it. The other assumes employees work because they want satisfaction, to belong to something and make a difference. Some employees fit the first assumption and others fit the second.

This realization makes hiring the right employees so much more important. If nothing else, the interview needs to try to discover why the candidate wants to work - what motivates him or her. The best training in the world will often fail to motivate an employee that is just putting in time.

Employees are investments. Every manager wants his or her investments to appreciate. A manager can get the most out of the employee (investment) by motivation. I do not want to ignore the importance of training rather focus on motivation. Management needs to make asserted efforts to motivate employees if it is to get the most of its investment in them.

Employees need to be appreciated. Too often employees are only told when they do something wrong. The good employee that makes few mistakes is often ignored. When an employee is appreciated he or she becomes motivated. The author recalls the experience of working in a restaurant while in college. One evening after a really busy dinner rush the manager came out and gave some of the workers a couple of tickets to a local theater and told them how much he appreciated the job they had done that night. Not only did that motivate them but it created a sense of loyalty to him and the restaurant.

The manager at that restaurant did more than show appreciation. He made the workers feel important. He never talked down to them. The author's job was to carve roast beef and ham. He had to satisfy the customers while looking out for the interests of the restaurant. That meant not cutting the meat too thick nor too thin. That manager made all the employees feel important. The cooks, bus-boys and even the dishwashers knew the restaurant could not function without them. In fact, they knew they affected the restaurant's bottom line. Each of them in that restaurant were part of a team because the management motivated them.

Managers must be concerned about the company. Part of being concerned about the company is being concerned about its employees. In many industries the employees are a large part of the company. Some managers that consider themselves "hard-nosed" or "tough" fail in their relationships with their workers and peers. That is not to suggest a "nice-guy" approach that compromises the company's interests. Quite to the contrary, employee motivation increases the strength and value of a company.

How does Paul's counsel of Ephesians 6:9 apply to managers of today? "And, ye masters, do the same things unto [servants], forbearing threatening: knowing that your Master also is in heaven; neither is there respect of persons with Him." Paul was then telling slave owners to treat their slaves with dignity and respect. Such counsel still applies to managers today. Each employee under our charge has as much right to job satisfaction as we do. We are charged with creating a positive environment for our employees.

A little praise can motivate many employees. Praise must not be confused with flattery. Flattery is insincere or excessive. Praise is a good word of encouragement. When a manager demands a lot from his or her employees, praise must be given just as freely as criticism. Jesus constructively criticized a lot. As we read the gospels we see Jesus rebuking people of every class. Jesus criticized priests, businessmen as well as His own disciples. We also see positive reinforcement. Upon healing an afflicted woman Jesus told her, "Daughter, be of good comfort; thy faith hath made thee whole." To the Canaanitish woman Christ said, "O woman, great is thy faith: be it unto thee even as thou wilt." To a certain lawyer He said, "Thou hast answered right: this do, and thou shalt live." This is the example Christ provided for us.

Listening Skills

Listening skills are an important part of business communication. James 1:19 says, "my beloved brethren, let every man be swift to hear, slow to speak, slow to wrath". Too many managers think too highly of their own opinions and are too quick to voice them. This will be discussed in greater detail in the next chapter.

Note Taking Skills

The ability to take notes comes with a few things. Experience teaches the manager what information most merits being noted. Notes should record who said what and what action is required. Recording meetings in addition to taking notes is best provided one has time to later go back and listen to the recording. Since time does not always allow one to do that, taking good notes the first time is still important. Digital voice recorders can also be helpful ways to take notes when one is driving or otherwise unable to use a notepad or some kind.

Ability to Help Others

How does the ability to help others increase the value of a manager? Helping others is compassionate. Christians are to be compassionate as Christ was compassionate. There should be little doubt that being more Christ-like will make a of any less value? Helping and enabling are distinctly different. When one person enables another, they are doing something for them. When that same person helps them, they assist them to do something.

In recent years enabling has gotten the bad name it deserves. If one person does another person's job for them why is that other person employed by the company? Is it for the best of the company for one to do another's job? Enabling not only does what someone else should be doing but it prevents them from learning from the experience. Enabling is beyond helping. Enabling will decrease the value of the person being enabled.

While helping someone, the one being helped continues to do his or her job, only with assistance. Helping someone often requires a manager to be meek. When helping someone the manager assists yet is not in charge. A manager often has to set aside something they are doing to help another. Helping another in most cases is unselfish. The sinner's nature calls him or her to act selfishly. How willing is one to help others? How can time management enable one to help others? Matthew 25:40 is clear on this duty: "Inasmuch as ye have done it unto one of the least if these my brethren, ye have done it unto Me."

Physical Appearance

The physical appearance of a manager should not be thought of as little importance. Managers should dress appropriate to their position. The old adage says "cleanliness is next to godliness". As Christians we are not called to wear expensive clothing, jewelry and perfumes. Our appearance should be neat, clean and simple. If our position calls for us to wear a tie or a uniform it should be clean and neat. Our appearance speaks for us and we are often judged by it.

There is also reason to believe the way a person dresses actually impacts their job performance. Telemarketers that are required to dress formally have been shown to be more successful than those that dress casually even though their clients can never see them. Students required to wear a school uniform also tend to have less behavior problems than those that are not. So our physical appearance is not a small issue.

Vocabulary Skills

Verbal skills are very important. This too is discussed in the next chapter. Christ said, "For by thy words thou shalt be justified, and by thy words thou shalt be condemned." If God considers speech so serious, how do our peers, employees and clients consider it? Speech does leave an impression with everyone in a manager's world.

The first impression is often made by a manager's verbal skills. Managers that struggle with this can join organizations like the Toast Masters or record themselves. Practicing a speech or presentation in front of the mirror can be helpful. A manager wants to project confidence and ability and that is often done through speech. One doesn't want to be heard whining or indecisive.

Non-verbal Skills

Non-verbal communication also leaves an impression. This too will be discussed in the next chapter. Some men have practiced making faces in a mirror. "Why?" the reader may ask. Because they want to know how they look to other people. Should everyone be that concerned about non-verbal communication? How does one look when in a boring business meeting? How does one look when holding in their anger? How does one look when giving a directive to someone? Non-verbal communication is understood by those about us.

Many times a manager cannot control his or her non-verbal expression. Control comes only by dealing with deeper issues. Non-verbal signals are often given by managers struggling with anger or anxiety. Managers excited about things going on in their personal lives can also send non-verbal signals in the work place they are unaware of. Personal Bible study and prayer have a way of helping a person deal with these deeper issues in the long term. Frequently there is no quick solution for managers whose deeper issues result in negative non-verbal expressions.

Proper Sleep at Night

Proper sleep impacts a manager's performance. There is a lot of truth to the old adage, "Early to bed, early to rise, makes a man healthy, wealthy and wise." When a manager stays up late and gets up early the cheat themselves and their company. That is not to say it is sinful to work on little sleep once in a while. However the manger owes it to his company to get an average of seven hours of sleep each night on a regular basis.

Fortune magazine reported lack of sleep is one of the most common reasons for reduced performance by managers. Mark Eppler in *Management Mess-Ups* wrote, "I derived a perverse pleasure in being the first one to arrive at work and the last one to leave... When the time came to 'pay the piper' for my transgressions, the price was severe. I battled chronic fatigue for nearly five years before regaining full strength." Some have the image of the fast-paced manager, working with six hours of sleep and a cup of coffee, as a model of a dedicated businessman. The fact is that such managers deprive their companies of efficiency and their best creativity when they skimp on sleep.

Laurie Beth Jones in her book, *Jesus Inc.*, points out the results of sleep deprivation in society. "Our ignoring of the concept of rest is taking its toll. High schools and colleges are spending enormous sums of money to educate students who are too sleepy to take in or analyze information. Drowsy drivers cause roughly 100,000 accidents each year. Research commissioned by the U.S. Congress indicated that lack of sleep led to errors in critical thinking in three of the worst disasters in recent U.S. history: the *Challenger* explosion, the *Exxon Valdez* oil spill, and the near-meltdown at *Three Mile Island*."

Legal Knowledge of My Industry

Most every industry in the United States is impacted by government regulations. Handicap accessibility codes, fire codes, labor laws and sexual-harassment laws affect almost all companies. Specific industries have additional laws that affect them. Knowledge of these laws can be obtained by attending classes and seminars, speaking with your company's lawyer, or by simply reading. Legal knowledge affects many decisions managers make.

Attitude

Attitude makes a big difference in every line of work. Life is 10% what happens and 90% the reaction to it. This is hard for some people to grasp so let's consider an illustration. One morning a man wakes up and goes out to get his morning paper. He finds his paper in his bushes instead of in driveway or on his front step. He chuckles to himself and thinks of how the paperboy is in such a hurry. The same thing happened with the man's neighbor. It irritated him terribly. He came into his house swearing and in a bad mood. He set his alarm early and got up early the next morning. He waited for the paperboy. The paperboy again passed on his bike and again threw the paper in the bushes. The neighbor came out of his house yelling at the boy. As the boy turned back to see the man he was struck and killed by a car backing out of a driveway. The neighbor said he was provoked to yell at the boy. He placed all the blame on the boy. If the boy had only thrown the paper in the right place he would have never yelled at him. Yet the boy did exactly the same thing to everyone on the block yet not everyone reacted in the same way.

So many people in this world today are guilty of this. They blame others for their reactions. They claim the circumstances are to blame for their lack of control. We find no biblical example to support such a belief. Christ was the perfect Example of self-control. As we start to see the world as Christ sees the world our attitudes will become more like His.

Self-control is the last of the fruits of the Spirit listed in Galatians 5:22, 23. The fruits are progressive so that means before one will gain self-control they will first gain all the fruits that come before it. "But the fruit of the Spirit is love, joy, peace, forbearance, kindness, goodness, faithfulness, gentleness and self-control. Against such things there is no law." All these fruits combine make for a very good attitude.

Ability to do Paperwork

The ability to keep up with paperwork is not accomplished just by working faster. If that is the chosen method the quality of work may well suffer. Being able to keep up with the workload is often related to the ability to delegate work to others and the ability to prioritize. If time is not being wasted on trivial matters, or company gossip at the water cooler, and one still cannot keep up with the paperwork they either need an assistant, need to quit doing what should be delegated or need to prioritize.

Ability to Prioritize

The reason many managers cannot keep up with their paperwork is because they don't like doing it. It is not a priority to them. The importance of paperwork varies from company to company. Each manager should know how important it is in their company and prioritize it as such. . Assigning each task on a "To Do" list a priority number can help a manager stay focused on the high-priority tasks. The fact that paperwork can be boring cannot be a reason a Christian manager falls behind in it

Continuous improvement means more than just doing what needs to be done each day. It means a manager evaluating him or herself on a regular basis. It means taking steps to improve performance and reduce errors. It means being humble and letting Christ be the Example. Continuous improvement should be a part of each Christian manager's work experience.

3

Communication

God communicated with man first face to face. God also communicates with man through the lessons of nature. He communicates with man through His Word. God sent His Son to communicate with man. He listens to man through prayer. God answers prayers. Business communication is not just about how to write letters and give speeches. Business communication, for a Christian manager, must start with learning how God communicates.

The Scriptures teach that God's means of communication varies depending upon the circumstances. God's means of communication depends upon the person He is communicating with, the circumstances and history. Examples of these communications are found throughout the Scripture from Genesis to Revelation. Let's look at the examples of Adam, Noah, Moses, Job, Daniel, Nebuchadnezzar, Belshazzar, the Pharisees and temple merchants and Paul.

God's first words to sinful man were, "Where art thou?" God was compassionate with Adam and Eve after the fall. He understood that while they had sinned against Him, they were deceived. While God spoke kindly to those who had hurt Him, His words were quite different for the serpent, "thou art cursed above all cattle... I will put enmity between thee and the woman, and between thy seed and her seed; it shall bruise thy head, and thou shalt bruise his head." These strong words were because the circumstances were different.

A manager ought to have compassion with those who are doing things wrong due to lack of training, experience or as a result of being purposely lead down the wrong path by another. Many will make short cuts they see other employees doing. While they know it isn't right they justify such action by the precedent set by others. Just as God asked sinful man, "Where are thou?", it would be quite appropriate for a Christian manager to ask such an employee, "What are you doing?"

A much less compassionate position needs to be taken with those purposely working against a company. There are those who regularly cheat the company by extending paid breaks from fifteen to twenty minutes. There are those who try to get away with doing as little as possible. There are those who embezzle valued company assets. Such actions require less compassion. It is note worthy that the serpent's violation in the garden was not its first. "There was war in heaven: Michael and His angels fought against the dragon; and the dragon fought and his angels... the great dragon was cast out, that old serpent, called the Devil, and Satan, which deceiveth the whole world" Revelation 12:7, 9. Ellen White wrote in *Patriarchs and Prophets* of how God first dealt with this rebellion. "The Son of God presented before him the greatness, the goodness, and the justice of the Creator, and the unchanging nature of His law... But the warning, given in infinite love and mercy, only aroused a spirit of resistance." (p. 36) When dealing with the serpent in the garden God knew there was no hope for his redemption.

26

In the story of Noah we find God used a man to communicate with others. God could have spoken directly to the world as He did to the Children of Israel at Mount Sinai. God chose to use Noah and He gave the world 120 years to accept His warning. The church was lost with the rest of the world. Genesis chapter two says, "the sons of God [believers] saw the daughters of men [non-believers] that they were fair; and they took them wives of all which they chose." A great responsibility was delegated to Noah. God knew that if they would not listen to Noah they wouldn't listen to Him either. It was as Christ stated in the parable of the rich man and Lazarus, "If they hear not Moses and the prophets, neither will they be persuaded, though one rose from the dead." (Luke 16:31)

Often a manager's best means of communication is through a delegated spokesman. In schools of management it is taught that responsibility must equal authority. While God gave Noah a great amount of responsibility He also gave him a great amount of authority. Noah was not chosen at random. Scripture says, "Noah found grace in the eyes of the Lord." Those who have authority delegated to them must be chosen with divine wisdom. This requires thoughtful prayer and meditation. Decisions of this nature should rarely be made in haste.

Moses is one of the few men we find in the Old Testament who spoke directly to God. Moses, like Noah, was a delegated spokesman. There are many lessons a manager can learn from the life of Moses. The Rebellion of Korah, recorded in Numbers 16, is a fine example of authority equaling responsibility. Korah built an alliance of renown men of Israel to question the authority of Moses. "Moses said, Hereby ye shall know that the Lord hath sent me to do all these works; for I have not done them of mine own mind." God first wanted to destroy the entire congregation that had allied itself with Korah. How many managers are that eager to stand behind those they have invested with authority? God was communicating a strong message to Israel and all after who may now learn from this story. When God places a man in a position of authority, that authority is to be respected. Remember, God does not choose these men at random.

Too often managers, and church leaders for that matter, try to micromanage tasks they have delegated. While a manager ought to follow up on delegated tasks to make sure they are being done, the authority to do the task must given to the individual just as the responsibility was. Those who try to micromanage delegated tasks eventually discover no one wants to volunteer to work with them. If a manger is not willing to grant a subordinate the authority to accomplish a task he or she should not give them the responsibility either.

The story of Moses striking the rock in Kadesh has a lesson in communications for managers. The Children of Israel were complaining, had little faith and blaming Moses for the poor conditions they were in. They were thirsty and in the desert. The Lord instructed Moses to speak to a rock and water would flow from the rock. Moses struck the rock with his rod instead of speaking to it. Moses was frustrated and not thinking about the lesson that speaking to the rock was to teach. Moses had struck a rock before for water. The rock represented Jesus. Being struck represented His suffering death. The lesson to be learned from Moses speaking to the rock was that Jesus only had to die once. The rock did not have to be smitten again. Moses was upset. He was not looking out for the interests of

God. His punishment was severe; the lesson is great. When authority is delegated to us we must not let emotions cause us to forget our purpose.

Job did not understand the great controversy between Christ and Satan. This is clear from his statement, "the Lord gave, and the Lord hath taken away." The Lord did give but it was Satan that took away. There is a lesson in communications in the life of Job. It is the lack of communication. God allowed the devil to injure Job and did not rush in to explain what was happening. What were the circumstances that caused God to leave Job in the dark for so long about what was going on? Edwin Thiele in the book *Job and The Devil* wrote, "With satanic subtlety and insinuation [Satan] charged that God purchased Job's fidelity with blessings. Thus, he also accused God of selfishness." If God allowed such an accusation to stand it may cause many to doubt Him and lose the blessing they would otherwise have. It was for the good of humanity that Satan's accusation be shown false. Job was told no more than he needed to know. What Job knew was enough.

This is a principle many Christian managers have to apply. Many times a manager wants to tell someone something but must withhold the information for the best of the company or others involved. Therefore only that which needs to be communicated is. Examples of such are pending layoffs, mergers, negotiations in progress, accounts receivables and payables. Sometimes compassion wants to tell someone if they are about to be terminated or if they are investing in a stock that is about to fall through the floor. It is likely that God wanted to tell Job what was going on in his life too. God governs His actions by principle and not emotion. Such is our Example.

Job also teaches us another lesson about how God communicates. The book starts with God in what seems to be a meeting with the sons of God. Knowing that God created other worlds (Hebrews 1:2) and that Adam was a son of God (Luke 3:38), it is believed these sons of God were representatives from other worlds. Satan showing up at this meeting, claiming to represent earth (Job 1:7), reinforces such a belief. Why would a perfect God govern by committee? It seems He values the opinions of others. The fact He allowed Satan to be part of such meetings tells of God's fairness and willingness to hear His opposition. Christian managers will follow such an Example.

Daniel was a young man when he was taken captive into a foreign and pagan country. The first chapter of Daniel tells that the young man "purposed in his heart that he would not defile himself with the portion of the king's meat". Daniel was determined to be loyal to God in the small things as well as the big things. Such is an example of the type of person God chose to communicate with directly. God could trust Daniel in every respect of Daniel's life. The latter half of Daniel is filled with prophecy shown to Daniel in vision. Daniel was very humble in his communications with others. Daniel was the second most powerful man in the world. He held his position even after the Babylonian empire was defeated. He served under four monarchs. His life should be a study for each wanting to be a Christian manager.

Daniel is one of only a few Bible characters that has none of his sins recorded yet we find no arrogance in his life. Daniel spent time each day consulting with

God. When the king asked him to interpret a dream, Daniel's humble response was, "The secret which the king hath demanded cannot the wise men, the astrologers, the magicians, the soothsayers, shew the king; But there is a God in heaven that revealeth secrets, and maketh known to the king". That God is still in heaven and still reveals secrets to men and women who seek Him.

Later when Daniel interpreted the dream of the tree for the same king Daniel was troubled. It was not with eagerness that Daniel interpreted the dream. Managers often have to give bad news to their subordinates. Often times, like king Nebuchadnezzar, they are well deserving of what they have coming to them. Notwithstanding, a Christian manager should like no pleasure in the misfortune of another. Such bad news should be given in a tactful manner as Daniel's example.

God communicated with king Nebuchadnezzar through Daniel and his three friends. God saw something valuable in the king that made Him have patience with him. God had destroyed other men for what seems to be lesser offenses. The Biblical account leads us to believe that Nebuchadnezzar died a converted, humble man. Sometimes managers also need to have patience with subordinates. How many subordinates have been fired by one firm only to go on to make another firm quite successful?

Belshazzar was Nebuchadnessar's grandson. Belshazzar had a full knowledge of his grandfather's experiences. God communicated with Belshazzar in a way that made his "knees smote against in another." Why did God communicate bad news to Belshazzar differently than He did to Nebuchadnessar? Scripture seems to indicate the transgressions of Belshazzar were greater. Belshazzar was in outright defiance to God. It seems as if Belshazzar was tempting God to do something. Belshazzar drinking wine in the golden vessels he knew were sacred and had been taken from the temple.

Some people behave in a way which seems to be "asking to be fired." These are people who not only ignore directives given to them by superiors but defy them. One must scratch their head sometimes after seeing what others have done. If such behavior is allowed to continue, without something drastic being done, no respect for authority would exist in the company. Therefore circumstances sometimes call for a drastic resolution like that of Belshazzar.

Many point to Christ's behavior in the temple as justification for anger. Christ cleansed the temple on two occasions - at the beginning of His ministry and at the end of it. Christ also denounced the Pharisees in a manner some consider hostile. Is there such a thing as justifiable anger? The answer is probably yes. Jesus gave us an example of it. Notice what caused Jesus to get angry and what did not. When Jesus was falsely accused and crucified, what was His reaction? "Father, forgive them; for they know not what they do." (Luke 23:34) Why did Christ get angry at the Pharisees and the temple merchants? The answer is simple. They were hurting others. Christ's anger was never selfish. Christ was angered when He saw others being hurt.

Man seems to be quite different. Men and women tend to get angry when they are hurt. Few get upset when the news reports of someone being murdered or robbed. While if it was a relative that was murdered or if we were robbed we would be irate. Justifiable anger is a dubious luxury at best. It is best for the

Christian manger to pray that they are able to walk in such a way as to avoid anger altogether. Managers don't need to get angry to solve problems.

God gave Saul of Tarsus a wakeup call. Paul's conversion was dramatic. While not as dramatic, the author recalls when taking college algebra for the second time. The professor invited any of student that needed help to come by his office. Expecting to get some tutoring the author went to his office. After presenting the situation to him, the professor informed him that he was a bad student. He said the author's problem was that he went into the class thinking he knew something about algebra. He further stated that if the author did the homework each night and asked questions in class his test scores would increase. He was right. It was a wakeup call. The author's test scores went from Ds and Fs to Cs and Bs.

Often times managers have subordinates that they see something valuable in but are headed in the wrong direction. 1 John 4:8 tells us that God is love. This is not only one of the many character traits of God. Love is the governing principle for everything God does. God's justice, anger and compassion are fruit of His love - not apart from it. While wakeup calls often come from people that are frustrated or impatient they can come from love for our fellowman or subordinates.

Listening Skills

Listening skills are lacking in many managers. Few universities teach such skills. Scripture tells us, "let every man be swift to hear, slow to speak, slow to wrath". Mary Ellen Guffey in her textbook, *Business Communication*, states that the average person listens with only 25 percent efficiency. "In other words, *we ignore, forget, distort, or misunderstand 75 percent of everything we hear*."

Guffey points out nine poor listening habits. 1. Reacting to the speaker's appearance and speech mannerisms 2. Failing to control distractions 3. Listening to evaluate rather than understand 4. Daydreaming and pretending to listen 5. Assuming the speaker wants input or advice 6. Avoiding listening to anything difficult 7. Waiting to jump in and grab the limelight 8. Pretending to understand 9. Listening for facts only.

When listening a manager needs to become actively involved with what the speaker's concerns are. A manager needs to devote that time to trying to understand what the speaker is trying to communicate. A manager ought to avoid reacting defensively. A good listener will tactfully have the speaker clarify what he or she is saying. A good listener should not try to do another task while listening. Listening is a task in itself.

Patience and tolerance are needed in order to be a good listener. In today's business world everything is so fast-paced that few want to slow down to actually listen. Good listeners must tolerate others communication problems. Some managers will speak indirectly or "beat around the bush". The listener than needs to clarify exactly what the speaker is trying to say. Some speakers speak softly, stutter or have other speech problems. These require more patience and tolerance on the part of the listener.

Often times taking notes while listening is a great aid to understanding and remembering what a speaker says. This takes time and more effort than many managers want to commit to listening. Many managers are really lazy listeners. This should not be the case for the Christian manager. The Christian manager should be "quick to hear". Note taking is a skill that is developed with time and practice. The skill is often developed by trial and error. I have often taken notes during meetings. Later when asked about a specific topic discussed in the meeting I found my notes lacking, while my notes on other topics were extensive and yet never needed.

Listening skills can really suffer during a conversation on the telephone. Many managers will continue to do other work while "listening" to the other party speak. Often such behavior detracts significantly from hearing and understanding everything that is said. Often times a listener does not want to be having a phone conversation and will respond however needed as to terminate the phone conversation. Some of the worst listening habits occur during phone conversations.

Some phone conversations are not worth listening to. Sometimes it is because they call at a bad time, they are trying to sell a product not needed or trying to get information that needn't be released. Honesty and tactfulness is the best policy. Being rude with a caller may reflect poorly on your company's reputation. A Christian manager can honestly say, "I'm sorry you have called me at a bad time." or "I'm sorry my company has no interest in your services at this time". Sometimes one will need to be firm and almost rude in order to get the message across. Such action should not be a Christian manager's first option but should not be ruled out either. Christ and the prophets have left us an example in such areas.

Defensiveness can be a blockade to communication. When listening to another we ought to be on guard not to become defensive. Often times one becomes defensive when he or she feels they are being accused of some wrong doing. This is our carnal nature raising its ugly head. When listening we want to clearly understand the speaker. If we are being accused of wrongdoing we can deal with that later. Our goal in listening is to understand what is being said. Examples of being defensive are saying such things as, "I can't believe you would say that." or "I resent your accusation". A good listener would tactfully say, "Let me understand, you believe I am at fault?" or "Are you suggesting I am to blame?" When a listener becomes defensive the free flow of communication becomes blocked.

The listener wants the speaker to feel comfortable speaking. Eye contact and other nonverbal communication will tell the speaker how interested one is in listening. Christian managers should give a speaker the attention required in order to listen or tell the speaker he or she hasn't the time to give. Many times a subordinate has been disciplined for doing something and says, "I told you I was going to do it." The superior then had replied, "I don't remember you telling me anything about it." Does that sound familiar? Too familiar for many. Are the subordinates always lying or are there managers that just don't listen good enough? Enough importance cannot be placed on listening skills.

Managerial Meekness

Most Christian managers spend much of their days dealing with those who are not Christians. Nonbelievers cannot be expected to be honest. Some managers act as if they are insulted when someone lies to them. When dealing with nonbelievers it can almost be expected that they will lie if it seems in their best interest to do so. That is why legal contracts are used. Those who do not know Christ are living for self. It should be expected that they would make decisions based on self and lie to cover up mistakes that would reflect badly upon themselves.

The only difference between Christians and non-Christians is that Christians have been forgiven and found a relationship with Christ. The Christian manager should not get some self-righteous attitude of "How dare you lie to me?" That very same Christian manager would likely do the same thing if it weren't for what Christ did for him or her. "For by grace are ye saved through faith; and that not of yourselves: it is the gift of God: Not of works, lest any man should boast" Eph. 2:8, 9. Jesus invited us to react as He would react. "Take My yoke upon you, and learn of Me; for I am meek and lowly in heart: and ye shall find rest in your souls." Matt. 11:29.

Webster's New World Dictionary 1967 edition defines meek as: "1. Patient and mild. 2. Tamely submissive; spiritless". This has caused problems with many. How can a manager be meek and effective? Who wants to hire a manager that is spiritless? The Greek word used in Matthew 11:29 is praos; it translates as gentle, humble or meek. I like the paraphrase found in the Contemporary English Version of the Bible. It says, "Take the yoke I give you. Put it on your shoulders and learn of Me. I am gentle and humble, and you will find rest."

A Christian manager should be gentle and humble. We are gentle in the aspect that we are slow to anger, we listen with an open ear, our speech is void of vulgarity and we are polite with our arguments. We are humble knowing that it is for the grace of God that we have what has been given to us. Being gentle and humble does not mean we allow others to lie and not be held accountable. Christ does not do such. It does not mean allowing others take advantage of us or our position in our company. Nor does it mean we the best is not required from our subordinates. It does mean we have patience with others. The Christian manager understands that not all have accepted the gift of salvation. As a result when someone lies to them they tend not to explode in a fit of anger. A Christian manager has self-control.

The authors of the book *Alcoholics Anonymous* wrote something worth repeating. "We realized that the people who wronged us were perhaps spiritually sick. Though we did not like their symptoms and the way these disturbed us, they, like ourselves were sick too. We asked God to help us show them the same tolerance, pity, and patience that we would cheerfully grant a sick friend. When a person offended us we said, 'This is a sick man. How can I be helpful to him? God save me from being angry. Thy will be done'" (P. 66, 67). These ex-drunks seem to have discovered something many professed Christians still lack. Those that harm us do not have a good relationship with Christ. If they did they would not be intentionally harming people. We need to take that into consideration when dealing with them.

The February 2001 issue of *Signs Of The Times* reported a study printed earlier in *US News & World Report*. The five-year study at the University of North Carolina-Chapel Hill and St. Joseph's University found more that half of workers studied were distracted by rude behavior. Such distractions resulted in the workers losing efficiency due to fuming about what happened. The study found a quarter of the workers purposely quit trying to do their best and twelve percent quit altogether. Being gentle and humble with our subordinates and associates is a win-win situation.

Ellen White, in *Counsels To Writers And Editors*, wrote, "The plan of Christ's teaching should be ours. He was plain and simple, striking directly at the root of the matter, and the minds of all were met." (P.56) Sometimes managers are too smart for their own good. When communicating with another a simple thing is made complicated. This happens when instructing an employee on how to do a new task or when trying to track a shipment that seems to be lost in freight. Christ did not "beat around the bush." Look at the conversation He had with Nicodmus in John chapter three or with Pilate in chapter 18. Jesus could have responded to these men's questions with a sermon but He kept His answers short and direct. Sometimes we speak simply to hear the sound of our own voice. Our Lord gave us no such example.

A good communicator must be humble. Although a listener should ask for clarification when he or she does not understand a speaker's message, the speaker is responsible that the listener understands. Some have an attitude that if the listener doesn't understand and isn't smart enough to ask questions it is their problem. A good communicator will have no such attitude. A good communicator will go the extra mile when speaking to make sure the listener understands what is being said.

Often times when a manager is asked why something has not been done the answer is that they told someone to do it. The reply "I told them" seems like a way for them to exit the question. It is as if they believe that once they delegate something to one of their subordinates they are no longer responsible to see it gets done. The problem is lack of communication. The manager delegating a task is not being understood. Either the subordinate does not understand what needs to be done, the priority of the task or the consequence of not doing it. The responsibility of being understood rests on the speaker. Therefore if someone is told to do something and it is not done, frequently it will come back to the manager who gave the instructions.

How should a humble manager go about setting an erring employee back on the right track? There can be no one rule to govern this. Some need only to be gently spoken to. Others will require an earth-shaking wake-up call. Some need to be fired. These are those that will not respond to any type of correction. "He that reproveth a scorner getteth himself shame: and he that rebuketh a wicked man getteth himself a blot. Reprove not a scorner, lest he hate thee: rebuke a wise man, and he will love thee." Prov.9:7, 8. One rule can be established. One should always seek guidance in prayer first.

Written Communication

Some managers do not like the paper trail. Some prefer to give all instructions and handle all conflict orally. Oral communication can be positive in many ways. The first is that it is personable. When two people can hear each others' voice the communication seems more friendly or non-friendly as the case may be. However oral communication is often misunderstood. Attitudes can interfere with such communication. When communicating with the written word a message cannot so easily be misunderstood. The one receiving the communication can read it while angry and later while calm. The receiver can take the communication to another and ask what the other thinks of it. Written communication is tangible. It can be held, copied, filed and used in litigation if needed.

Combining both forms is often best. A manager speak with another in person or by telephone and afterwards follow it up with an e-mail to confirm what we discussed. This gives the personality of oral communication with the benefits of written communication. Sometimes a manager is unable to get a hold of someone to speak with him or her. Under such circumstances they are left only the option of written communication. When such is the case the manager should have a return receipt on the email that will confirm it was delivered and opened.

Written communication needs to be filed and kept in most cases. This gets into filing. Our God is a God or order. The book of nature teaches us how organized God is. It is no wonder where the saying "Cleanliness is next to godliness" came from. All too often a manager is unable to find a document that he or she has filed. One's filing system should be done in such an order that one's associate or secretary could find a needed file.

There are managers that rarely use written communication because they claim they didn't have time for it. This is perhaps less true today than in the past due to the prevalence of email and smart phones. However those types of managers still exist. They make various phone calls, placing demands and expectations on others and never have any evidence to show. When deadlines are not met and tasks not done correctly, all they can say is "I told them." Written communication enforces that which is said.

A teenager may receive various oral warnings from a boss. When the boss sits them down and gives them a written warning they know they are in trouble. It doesn't take years of experience in the workplace to get that message. When we put something in writing it becomes more valid. It is a mistake to think we need only speak and what we say will be understood, remembered and done.

Body Language

Christ set such a humble example for us to follow. He never took on an attitude that He was of a higher class than others - although He was. His treatment of others was never determined by their income or social status. The Christian manager should not allow such things to determine his or her treatment of others either.

Body language will often convey what one is feeling. One can easily observe another speaking while frustrated, disappointed, angry and shocked. While the words they use may not identify these feelings, their body language does. One can see condensing body language. The words do not elevate the speaker above the listener although the body language does.

If we are going to be good communicators we must first accept the example Christ gave us and choose it to be our own. This is not easy for the prideful. *The attitude that we are self-made and somehow pulled ourselves up by our boot-straps must be abandoned.* We are what we are but for the grace of God.

A manager's employees and associates make up his or her team. His or her body language must be consistent with other forms of communications. If employees are treated like the manager would like to be treated if our roles were reversed, they are more likely to feel like a respected team member. When they have accepted their role on the team a valued employee has been gained.

The richest man the author ever met was a Christian businessman. He met him at a Christian academy during a multi-church function. It was informal and the wealthy man was wearing striped overalls. They spoke about Christian education and went their separate ways. It was later the author learned who the man was and that he was worth hundreds of millions. What was so profound about it was that the wealthy man spoke to the author and listened as if I was his peer - his equal – and gave no hint of who he was. The author was just a poor student at the time. The wealthy man had accepted the example of Christ and made it his own.

Prayer

Most Christians do not pray as often as they should. This holds true for Christian managers too. While it may not be more important for Christian managers to pray than others, it certainly is no less important. In *Testimonies to Ministers & Gospel Workers* Ellen White wrote, "But frequently when placed in high positions of trust, men fail to take time to pray; they think they have no time to train their every faculty to respond to the convictions of the Holy Spirit. But if these men would sit at the feet of the meek and lowly Jesus they would... rend God to God the sacrifice of a noble, self-denying, cross-bearing life" (p. 283).

While each manager needs to pray for guidance and direction in the decisions one must make throughout the day, Roger Morneau points out in his book, *The Incredible Power of Prayer*, more reason than that. He wrote, "I became deeply impressed with the thought that God was calling me to do a work that not even the angels of heaven could do. He wanted me to be an intercessor for the unsaved and the ungodly that I met in my work." (P.41) Managers work with many unbelievers that will never be in a church. Some people go through all of life without anyone ever praying for them.

We know that Satan claims this world as his. His answer to God in the first chapter of Job is evidence of that as well as the third great temptation of Christ in the wilderness. He said, "I will exalt my throne above the stars of God: I will sit also upon the mount of the congregation, in the sides of the north: I will ascend above the heights of the clouds; I will be like the most High" The Bible makes the

Great Controversy between Christ and Satan clear. As managers we are in a part of this spiritual battle that many ministers will never reach. While managers may not be ministers or preachers, they are called to be gospel workers in this world claimed by Satan.

Some places of business do not allow employees to speak of religion. However they cannot forbid them from praying for one another. There are some workers that it would not be prudent to speak to about Christ but we can pray for them. It is very important to pray for those who seem to be working against us. We ought to pray they receive everything we want. If it be a new home, car, health, promotion or the like. Praying for others will cause us to come a little closer to having the mind of Christ.

The more we pray the more we will do business as Christ would do business. While some may frown on us for that it, others will have eternal rewards. Once inside heaven's gates we will discover how many were influenced by our example - for good and for bad.

Meditation

Jerry Bridges writes in *The Pursuit of Holiness*, "It is hypocritical to pray for victory over our sins yet be careless in our intake of the Word of God." "We need a planned time each day for reading or studying the Bible. Every Christian who makes progress in holiness is a person who has disciplined his life so that he spends regular time in the Bible. There simply is no other way" (p.78, 101)

Meditation is listening to God. This is a communication skill that too many slack off on. Listening to a sermon once a week is not enough. Satan will sift those who profess to be Christians, but do not spend daily time with the Bible, as wheat. This is why Satan will present to us a hundred reasons to put off the study of God's Word. Satan stands much to lose when we incline our ear to God.

The more time we spend in meditation the better we get to know Jesus. Jesus becomes a better friend. We start to understand how He would handle situations that we must face. Our prayers become much more effective. As we pray the Holy Spirit can bring to mind passages of Scripture that will answer just the problem we are facing. If we fail to study Scripture the passages will not be there for the Holy Spirit to bring to mind.

As meditation brings us closer to God we learn just how far away we are. Spending time with God will make us humble and wise. "My son, if thou wilt receive My words, and hide My commandments with thee; so that thou incline thine ear unto wisdom, and apply thine heart to understanding; Yea, if thou criest after knowledge, and liftest up thy voice for understanding; If thou seeketh her as silver, and searchest for her as for hid treasures; Then shalt thou understand the fear of the Lord, and find the knowledge of God. For the Lord giveth wisdom: out of his mouth cometh knowledge and understanding."

Businessmen and women are to be as aggressive in their Bible study as they are in the business world. The proverb says, "seekest her as silver, and searchest for her as for hid treasures". I have found the two are tied together. The more I dedicate myself to meditation with God, the more I dedicate myself to my business. God wants me to be a successful businessman. His definition of success may be quite different from that of the world but is success nonetheless. The closer I get to Him and more time I spend with Him, the greater becomes the success He has for me.

Games

Most every corporate environment has its employees that engage in games. When one is not being open and honest in communication with another a game is being played. The message trying to be sent is hidden and not directly said. Christian managers should not play such games with others - obviously. The Bible instructs us to say what we mean. "Let your yea be yea; and your nay, nay" James 5:12. Yet Christian managers must deal with such games continuously.

Games are no good for a company. They often cause hard feelings. Frustrated workers reduce efficiency. Time is wasted in such games that could be better spent. Those participating in such games are trying to feel superior to the peers or get out of doing work. There are no noble motives to game playing.

There are some things a Christian manager may do to cause and/or prevent game playing. When a manager is overbearing, employees are more likely to engage in game playing. A stressful workplace also causes some to play games. Many who play games are not aware of what their motives are. It may take some observation to find the reason and an effort to do something about it. Books like Eric Berne's *Games People Play* describes many games a manager can look out for. When employees quit playing games more honest communication will result. Employees will trust each other more. Employees will work together better. The company will benefit.

Many games involve manipulation. Manipulating is often confused with persuading. The job of a manager is to manage people which means to get them to do what they are suppose to do. Persuading people is the act of honestly convincing them to do what we want them to do. The key word there is "honestly". Manipulating is the act of using deception or unfair tactics to get someone to do what we want them to do. Choosing to manipulate people is the opposite of trusting God. When we trust God, we make our case honestly and trust God with the results. When we manipulate we are placing our trust in our tactics and thus in ourselves. God uses honesty but Satan is the father of lies (John 8:44).

An example of manipulating is promising an employee a bonus if they will do something without the intention of ever giving it. In the book "Manipulation" by June Hunt, she also lists, "The religious employer who micromanages employees, expecting them to work long hours without equitable monetary compensation" as an example of manipulation.

June Hunt lists methods used by manipulators.
- Say anything to humiliate
- Dominate conversation to get control
- Scold others to make them feel sad
- Blame others to make them feel bad

- Play the "guilt" game to make others at fault
- Shame others to make them feel sorry
- Play the victim to make others feel obligated
- Assist others to gain a sense of indebtedness
- Praise others to gain approval
- Use charm to gain favor of others
- Do kind acts to gain loyalty

Some of these methods are clearly bad while others are good deeds with strings attached. The Christian manager wants to make sure to avoid using all forms of manipulation because, first of all, God commands us to deal honestly with others. Then too, those that are being manipulated tend to rebel eventually. If we want our career in management to actually be a ministry, manipulation will completely undermine it. The example of manipulation gives teaches people to trust in themselves rather than God.

Small Talk and Shoptalk

There is a line of thinking that believes small talk and sometimes shoptalk is a waste of time. Small talk is when employees speak to each other about family, sports, politics, religion or some other issue outside of the industry they are working in. Shoptalk is when employees speak to each other in a casual manner about issues within their respective industries. Neither has a direct positive impact on productivity. For that reason some managers frown on permitting it.

However there is reason to believe both small talk and shoptalk can have an indirect positive impact on productivity so long as it is not excessive. This type of sharing between employees can boost company moral by creating a positive corporate environment. Such a result not only can increase employee efficiency, since happy workers normally work better, but can decrease turnover. Turnover, of course, costs the company in training and lost efficiency. This type of communication between employees can also cause them to feel like they belong to something. Employees can see each other as individuals and not just as the label of their respective positions.

What is excessive is something that is apt to vary from industry to industry and company to company. Small talk or shoptalk shouldn't go on much more than five minutes. When it starts stretching into ten or twenty minutes it seems more like a break or an all-out visit. Most of the times it should last about two or three minutes.

This type of communication on outside jobs typically will take place at the water cooler. In offices it typically takes place in the copy room. It happens when one employee passes another employee, both are busy doing something but take a moment to speak to each other. A manager may think he or she is improving productivity to holler at them to get back to work, but to do so may well impact productivity but not in the way the manager is hoping to. A discontent worker is not likely to go back to work energetic. Discontented workers are more likely to cause problems and quit. If the exchanges seem excessive it is best to speak to the individuals separately, explaining what one considers to be excessive, and try to monitor them in that regard.

Gossip

Gossip is a sin. We should not fool ourselves on the issue. The Bible is abundantly clear. "He that uttereth a slander, is a fool." "A froward man soweth strife: and a whisperer separateth chief friends" "The words of a talebearer are as wounds, and they go down into the innermost parts of the belly." "He that goeth about as a talebearer revealeth secrets: therefore meddle not with him that flattereth with his lips." "Where no wood is, there the fire goeth out: so where there is no talebearer, the strife ceaseth." Proverbs 10:18; 16:28; 18:8; 20:19; 26:20

When repeating something negative about another we ought to always ask ourselves some questions. Does repeating this information somehow help the person I am talking about? Whose interest does it serve to repeat this information? Is the motive for repeating this information to help someone or prevent some type of loss? Can I achieve the same goal by not mentioning the person the information is related to? Is the source of the information reliable or is it hearsay?

Sin is the breaking of God's law. However all infractions of the law are due to selfishness. Gossip is done so one can feel better than another, or in many cases it is done for entertainment or to actually due damage to the object of the gossip. There are valid reasons to speak about others while they may not be present. Simply speaking negatively of another when they are not present does not constitute gossip.

Let's look at the case of an alcoholic employee. Members of management may talk about him or her in regards on how the person may be used more efficiently, how the person may be disciplined, get professional help or discharged. Discussing the person's alcohol problem as it relates to the company's business is a legitimate concern and not gossip.

It should go without saying that King Solomon, inspired by the Holy Spirit, was much wiser than us when he wrote the book of Proverbs. Dealing with this issue is hard for most of us if we are going to be honest in so doing. This is because most of us take pleasure in character assassination all too often. The devil is "the accuser of brethren" and Christ said by our words we will be judged. Rev. 12:10. So this should not be an issue we only briefly think about.

Often times we consider sins such as murder, theft, drug dealing, prostitution, homosexuality, adultery, kidnapping and rape in a high class of sin. Other sins such as lying, swearing, Sabbath-breaking, pre-material sex, disrespecting one's parents and child neglect we tend to put into a middle class of sin. We consider sins such as class envy, gossip, gluttony, slothfulness and spiritual neglect small sins.

These small sins can easily affect the way we do business, our relationships with others and our relationship with God. While eating too much cake seems clearly a much smaller sin than selling a 15-year-old girl for sex, it does not go unnoticed by God or Mother Nature. Our bodies reap the results of our abuse. Solomon said gossip does damage to the inner most parts. While gossiping is not as bad as conning a retiree out of their life savings, we cannot escape the damage it does to that person and our reputation. *We must see all sin as grievous,* no matter how small it may be. If the only sin we ever committed was gossip we would still need a Savior.

The author had the unpleasant experience of working in a toxic environment due to gossip. It was a small construction company with about thirty employees. The office manager was a terrible gossip and talked bad about everyone – including the boss. She would always do it when they were not present and she had all the workers talking bad about each other. She would pit one against the other. She would inform the boss of juicy details and even had him paranoid of employees taking advantage of him. It was like some sort of dysfunctional family gone mad. The author started looking for another job almost as soon as he started. No one wins in an environment like that.

Resentment

Resentments are communicated to those about us in various ways. It has been said a man with resentment is like one with cancer. If it goes untreated it will prove fatal. Resentment will grow and grow until it manifests itself in an ugly manner. It doesn't take long before the resentment controls the man and not the man the resentment.

The word resentment comes from Latin. Sentment comes from the Latin word meaning to feel. Re is used to indicate multiple times. The words reoccur, recycle, rename, redo and remodel are such examples. Resentment then means to refeel. We resent someone when we refeel the pain, embarrassment, loss or other negative thing they caused us.

Interesting enough no one causes us to resent him or her. We are the root of all our resentments. When someone hurts us we feel bad, perhaps we get angry. Such a reaction is not resentment. It is a response to being hurt, embarrassed or experiencing loss. Paul warns us not to allow such a reaction to become resentment. "Be ye angry, and sin not: let not the sun go down upon your wrath" (Eph. 4:12) While there is such a thing as justifiable anger, there is no such thing as a justifiable resentment. Paul goes on to tell us how to prevent anger from becoming resentment. "Let all bitterness, and wrath, and anger, and clamor, and evil speaking, be put away from you with malice: And be ye kind one to another, tenderhearted, forgiving one another, even as God for Christ's sake hath forgiven you." (Ibid. 5:31-32)

How can one be "tenderhearted" with one who has hurt them? Simple. Those who have healthy relationships with Christ do not go around purposely hurting others. Therefore when someone hurts us it is normally safe to assume they do not have a healthy relationship with Christ. They are therefore spiritually sick. It is much easier for us to have compassion and be tenderhearted with those that are ill. Those with spiritual illness need our forgiveness and not our resentment.

It is important for the Christian manager to understand these things. Resentment profits no company's environment or any managers ability to think, reason and be productive. It certainly does not provide a healthy example of Christian love to others within one's influence.

We cannot always be sure whom we are influencing. The way we communicate to others is a witness to who our God is. Christians are judged by many. Our communication skills are not the least of things that we are judged by. A Christian manager should not be content with poor communication skills. We live in a world filled with resources. We worship a God able to make us wise. Managers have visible positions within their respective companies. God wills each of us to do His bidding.

4

Planning

"The World On Time" is Federal Express' slogan. It reflects the reality of business today. A business that is going to thrive will have to perform on schedule. Wholesalers must ship merchandise to retailers upon demand. Restaurants must deliver prepared food to waiting customers in a timely manner. Mechanics must repair cars on time. Pharmacists must fill prescriptions while customers shop. Manufacturers must deliver products faster than their competitors. Almost every kind of business must work with schedules. The ability to plan and schedule helps define the value of a manager.

The lack of planning will cause one to needlessly rush to accomplish some task at a later time. Often the task being done under the "rush" circumstances suffers. Things are not done as they should be and someone is left to explain why.

While in college the author went on a mission trip to El Salvador to help with the construction of some orphanages. After getting orientated into the position he came to understand the project was behind and over budget. He later learned that projects that are behind are often over budget. The project manager constantly had to handle little emergencies that were always popping up. Native workers were working late hours and keeping volunteers up. When he asked to see the project schedule he was ignored. Freshmen and sophomores are taught how to put together simple project schedules and much of the project manager's problems came from his lack of planning.

There are many examples of planning in the Scriptures. A portion of this chapter will examine some of them. The first is the death of Lazarus. After hearing of Lazarus' illness John records, "When He had heard therefore that he was sick, He abode two days still in the same place where He was." John 11:6. There are a few components to a plan. Christ had many options. He could have left at once and healed Lazaras. He could have healed Lazaras without leaving. He could have never left and never done anything. He chose to let Lazaras die and to raise him back to life. After evaluating each of the options a planner must decide which option will most likely achieve the end desired. In the case of Lazaras, Christ stated the goal was "that the Son of God might be glorified". Clearly Christ chose the option to best achieve this goal.

Some industries require more planning than do others. Many industries must plan research & development, shipping, marketing, inventory control, production, personnel leave and many other tasks. Not all planning requires a written schedule although all written schedules require planning. A plan is not something that is unchangeable. A plan can change as circumstances change. Often times a plan may anticipate various circumstances that may occur. Even if a plan must change it will still serve as a gage so the manager will know the status of whatever the given task.

Galations 4:4 confirms God had a plan. "When the fulness of the time was come, God sent forth His Son". It is also interesting that God made a schedule for this event. The schedule we find in Daniel chapter nine. "Know therefore and understand, that from the going forth of the commandment to restore and to build Jerusalem unto the Messiah the Prince shall be seven weeks, and threescore and two weeks: the street shall be built again, and the wall, even in troubles times. And after threescore and two weeks shall the Messiah be cut off, but not for Himself: and the people of the prince that shall destroy the city and the sanctuary; and the end thereof shall be with flood, and unto the end of the war desolations are determined. And He shall confirm the covenant with many for one week: and in the midst of the week He shall cause the sacrifice and the oblation to cease..."

Many that have studied prophecy are familiar with this but lets take a look at it again. The schedule has a starting point "the commandment to restore and to build Jerusalem". The command (mentioned in Ezra 6:14) was given in 457 BC and thus we have the starting point. The schedule also has a timeline. (In prophecy one day is considered a year. (See Num. 14:34; Ezek. 4:6) "Unto the Messiah shall be seven weeks, and threescore weeks and two weeks". Forty nine years (seven prophetic weeks) after the command to rebuild Jerusalem the reconstruction was completed. It came in right on schedule - just as God had outlined. 434 years later (62 prophetic weeks) Jesus was baptized. This was done as Paul wrote, "When the fulness of time was come". God's schedule then goes into the destruction that took place to Jerusalem in 70 AD before returning to the ministry of Christ. Christ ministered to the Jews for seven years (one prophetic week). First in person and then through His Apostles. In the middle of this ministry Christ was crucified thus causing "the sacrifice and oblation to cease."

	Jerusalem Restoration			Ministry To The Jewish People			
Command to Rebuild Jerusalem BC 457		Restoration Completed BC 408		Messiah Anointed AD 27	Messiah Cut Off AD 31	Apostles Preach & Heal	Gospel To The Gentile AD 3
		432 Years					
	49 Years			3.5 Years		3.5 Years	

At the end of this ministry Stephen was stoned and Saul of Tarsus was called to preach unto the Gentiles.

The Bible is filled with prophetic schedules of events that have passed and are yet to come. It is one thing to have a plan and yet another to have a schedule. A schedule allows others to see the plan and in many cases become part of it. God sets an example for us as an organized God. God not only knows the end from the beginning because He knows all but also because He makes plans and follows through with them.

It is also noteworthy that God placed men in positions of responsibility in regard to His plans. There are several examples of this in the Scripture starting with Noah. Noah was given the responsibility of building the ark and warning the world. Joseph was given the responsibility of storing grain for the years of famine. Moses was given the responsibility of the exodus. David was given the responsibility of expanding Israel. Solomon was responsible for building the temple. Later Ezra and Nehemiah were directed to rebuild it. Christ was responsible for His ministry and John the Baptist for preparing the people for it. Paul was responsible for taking the gospel to the Gentiles. Martin Luther and other reformers were responsible for bringing the church out of the Dark Ages. God did not select these men at random. These were men of trust and responsibility.

If a manager wants to see a plan come together he or she must place someone of trust and responsibility in charge of it. When we randomly place men and women in charge of a plan we are taking a gamble. Regardless of how well thought out the plan is or how structured and easy to read the schedule was made, if the person in charge of making it happen is inadequate it is unlikely things will go as planned. Sometimes additional education or assistance is required so that the plan becomes plausible.

The story of Jonah gives us another lesson in God's planning. Jonah preached, "Yet forty days, and Nineveh shall be overthrown." Today's English Version paraphrases as, "Forty days from now, Nineveh will be destroyed!" God had a definite plan to destroy the city. By letting others see this plan He allowed them to become part of it. In this case, part of changing it. Today's English Version paraphrases it like this, "When God saw that the people had stopped doing evil things, He had pity and did not destroy them as He had planned."

God has a back-up plan. His plan had a provision in it for a change in circumstances. A good Christian manager will also make back-up plans in case things do not progress as expected. This does not means the original plans are not rigorously pursued to prevent having to use the back-up plan. Unlike God's plan with Nineveh, most managers do not want to use the back-up plan.

Procrastination is a manager's nightmare. We must each come to the understanding that time is, in most cases, not our friend. The Earth does not stop its rotation around the Sun or spinning on its axis no matter how much we have to do. The clock does not consider those about him before allowing its hands to move forward. As time progresses our bodies age, our cars rust, weather abuses our houses, the sea eats our coast, food rots, nations' infrastructures deteriorate and all mortal life passes onto death. Time is the great equalizer. The rich and poor, educated and ignorant, city and rural areas all have the same amount of time. One of the greatest things about the next world is that there will be no time. We will no longer have to fight the clock. Yet while we are here we do have to fight the clock and procrastination squanders precious minutes, hours and days.

In Proverbs 3:28 we find this: "Say not unto thy neighbor, Go, and come again, and tomorrow I will give; when thou hast it by thee." Directly taken, this is telling us to pay our bills on time when we have the money to do so. It can also be understood as instruction not to procrastinate. The old adage, "Do not put off to tomorrow what can be done today." falls right in line with what Proverbs is telling us about paying bills.

The word procrastination normally has a bad condensation to it. The word simply means delay. While not all delays are thought of as being bad, most consider procrastination always to be bad. Most understand procrastinate as delaying that which should not or does not need to be delayed. As procrastination is discussed here, the latter understanding is that which the reader should use.

The procrastinator creates many of his or her problems. Tasks that are delayed are often done later without the ample amount of time for them to be done quickly. The procrastinator than must make up for his or her organizational skills with excuse-making skills. Had the tasks been done earlier, enough time would have been afforded and a better job would have been the result. While Proverbs 1:31 isn't necessarily speaking to the procrastinator it does apply. "Therefore shall they eat of the fruit of their own way, and be filled with their own devices."

Most procrastinators are either lazy, have their priorities mixed up or a little of both. For this reason the Christian manager needs to constantly be depending on Christ. Remember His words, "I am the vine, ye are the branches: He that abideth in Me, and I in him, the same bringeth forth much fruit: for without Me ye can do nothing." John 15:5. Some may need to speak with others they can trust about how to manage their time. "Where no counsel is, the people fall: but in the multitude of counselors there is safety." "He that walketh with wise men shall be wise: but a companion of fools shall be destroyed." "Hear instruction, and be wise, and refuse it not." Prov. 11:14; 13:20; 8:33.

God will place the people and tools in the life of the Christian manager to manage time if asked. "If ye then, being evil, know how to give good gifts unto your children, how much more shall your Father which is in heaven give good things to them that ask Him?" "If any of you lack wisdom, let him ask God, that giveth to all men liberally, and upbraideth not and it shall be given him." "When wisdom entereth into thine heart, and knowledge is pleasant unto thy soul; Discretion shall preserve thee, understanding shall keep thee" Matt. 7:11; James 1:5; Proverbs 2:10, 11. Proverbs 2:11 in Today's English Version is paraphrased to say, "Sound judgment and good sense will watch over you.." Sound judgment and good sense is what every Christian manager needs.

Today's world is filled with tools for time management. There is computer software with alarms and scores of aps that can be downloaded onto tablets and smart phones. Before any lack of planning is excused due to lack of technology lets remember that many great things were planned out and accomplished before today's technology. Let's just list a few to think about: Noah's ark, the pyramids, the Panama Canal, the railroads, many inventions including the electric light and submarine, and nearly all of history's wars. For each of these accomplishments many meetings were held and hundreds of deadlines were met or missed. A great amount of planning was accomplished without Microsoft or Motorola. While today's technology can be of tremendous use, lack of it is no excuse for lack of planning.

There is a great need for Christian managers to spend more time in prayer regarding decisions that are made. "Trust in the Lord with all thine heart, and lean not unto thine own understanding. In all thy ways acknowledge Him and He shall direct thy paths." "Pray without ceasing" Prov. 3:5, 6; 1 Thess. 5:17 A paraphrase of 1 Thessalonians 5:17 says, "never stop praying". Paul is directing Christians to constantly be in a mode of depending on Christ and looking for His guidance.

Sinful humans can so easily be fooled by the enemy. Christ is not only our best hope; He is our only hope. Who else will best lead a manager to choose the right marketing campaign, who to lay off, who to hire, which insurance company to use, which contracts to pursuit, etc.?

Some readers may be thinking, "How will Christ direct me in business decisions? The Bible says nothing about my industry." The Bible gives us abundant evidence that God works through people. That is why it is so important to walk with the wise and have a multitude of counselors. Most of all never stop praying! "Wisdom is the principle thing; therefore get wisdom: and with all thy getting get understanding... Get wisdom, get understanding: forget it not" Prob. 4:7, 5. The Christian manager will remain humble as s/he continuously seeks God's will.

It appears one of the chief reasons for the lack of planning is laziness. It is unfortunate when a competent manager, knowledgeable in his or her industry fails to plan simply because they don't feel like it. Many times I have heard excuses that time spent planning is a waste of time or that one doesn't have enough time to plan. The fact is that planning is an excellent use of time that will repay itself with great interest. Sadly the real reason many fail in planning is pure laziness.

The Scripture condemns laziness. "He becometh poor that dealeth with a slack hand: but the hand of the diligent maketh rich." "The hand of the diligent shall bear rule: but the slothful shall be under tribute." "The soul of the sluggard desireth, and hath nothing: but the soul of the diligent shall be made fat." "The way of a slothful man is as an hedge of thorns" "He that is slothful in his work is brother to him that is a great waster." Prob. 10:4; 12:24; 13:4; 15:19; 18:9

Why is the slothful man a brother of a great waster? The slothful is wasting time. Time is that precious commodity that scheduling is to increase. Business schools are known for teaching that failing to plan is planning to fail. Every manager plans. They either plan for success or plan for failure. It has been said that there are three types of managers. Those that make things happen, those that let things happen and those that say, "What happened?"

There is no honor in letting things happen. God did not create this world, set it spinning and go unto His next project. God has been active in human affairs every since He breathed into Adam's nostrils. The salvation of humanity is only one of the great accomplishments God has done throughout this planet's history. A Christian manager will follow such an Example. While we are not God and cannot be as involved with everything under us as He is, we shouldn't just let things happen.

Schedules often delegate tasks to subordinates. When subordinates fail to complete tasks delegated to them they do not always deserve all the blame. Let's look at an example. Jack runs a small chain of restaurants. Mother's Day had always been the busiest day of the year. Jack decided to plan out this Mothers' Day activities. Jack held a meeting with a group of managers. Rick was put in charge of a marketing campaign. Troy was put in charge of purchasing the needed food for a special menu item. Mark was put in charge of scheduling the employees. Jack went on running the business from the central office. When Mothers' Day came it was a disaster. Rick had advertised a prime rib special.

Troy was unaware of what was being advertised until Wednesday. No prime rib was available on such short notice. Mark had scheduled a new cashier to work the lunch hour. The cashier was overwhelmed and all the customers wanted prime rib. While Jack wanted to blame his management team, he knew he could have prevented the disaster by making sure tasks were done and coordinated.

Frequently managers play a vital role in making tasks come in on schedule. The responsibility of the part one must do should not be taken lightly. Staying on schedule is almost as important as quality in many industries. If the portion of work delegated to a manager becomes too much, something should be said while others' help might have a significant impact. Many do no ask for help until it is too late to avoid the inevitable. Pride is often to blame. The Christian manager cannot afford such an unworthy companion. Self-sufficiency and pride must be disposed of each morning. "the warfare against self is the greatest battle that was ever fought" is perhaps the most famous quote from Ellen White's book *Steps To Christ*.

To neglect a schedule is much like falling asleep at the wheel. In such cases someone or something else takes control. In a sermon about Jonah, Joe Crews is quoted as saying, "A worldling is ahead of a sleeping Christian." While Jonah was sleeping, the heathens on board were praying. When morning prayer is neglected and the Christian managers slips into a "spiritual sleep" the job performance suffers.

A schedule allows each participant to see the big picture. The attitude of some managers is that the subordinates need to do what they are told without asking questions. Some feel the subordinate needn't see the big picture rather just do what they are told. There are circumstances where that is true. I think of the story of Abraham sacrificing his son. God did not let him in on the big picture. God commanded him to do it and Abraham was to obey. However there are many more situations where God made great attempts to show us the big picture.

The sanctuary service was great in detail to teach man the intricate details of the plan of salvation. The Sabbath commandment explains why the day is to be kept holy, "For in six days the Lord made heaven and earth, the sea and all that in them is, and rested on the seventh day". God could have required blind trust and faith but He gave more.

When an employee or a subcontractor can see the big picture he or she is more likely to be motivated to play their part. They are less likely to waiver from instructions given. They are likely to feel that they are part of something and that management appreciates them. Positive attitudes are worth the few extra minutes that it may take to explain the big picture or the cost of printing out an additional schedule. Such attitudes can reduce turnover and increase efficiently.

An effective plan prevents crisis management, helps keep projects in budget, allows everyone to be informed and repays itself with interest. Such planning is a result of choosing between options. Divine guidance is available through prayer. When a schedule is made it allows a manager to gage progress and use time as a precious asset. Planning and scheduling are a part of today's business world no less than they have been throughout history. God is able to make each manager wise as he or she submits to Him.

5

Customer Service

"The customer is always right" is what we have been taught and told ever since forever. The customer is always right because without the customer there is no revenue and the business fails. Therefore the business must always search for a means to appease its customers. The silent customer is said to be the most dangerous. This is the customer that never complains about service or products. After making the purchase and not being satisfied he or she simply does not patronize the business. He or she will often relay the bad experience to family and friends but never to the business itself. Such a client does not allow the business to take corrective action to correct the wrong. Yet most dissatisfied customers fall into this category. Most dissatisfied customers do not return merchandise or demand better service. That is why it is so important that every customer has a good taste in his or her mouth at the end of each transaction.

Paul Timm, in his book *50 Powerful Ideas You Can Use To Keep Your Customers,* states one unhappy customer can cause a business to lose 67 of their customers! He also points out that in retail it costs an average of $19 to keep a customer happy as compared to an average of $118 to get a new customer. A business cannot afford to have employees that do not value each and every customer.

Somehow this information does not flow from business schools to managers and then to workers themselves. Many workers actually think their wages come from their boss or the large company they are employed by. They don't follow the money the short distance to the customer. Workers often treat the customer as if he or she is an annoyance they must put up with. This is an attitude not only in retail stores but also in wholesalers and manufacturers! It is also found in hospitals and government offices. It is imperative for the Christian managers to not only instruct employees of customer service but to lead by example.

While studying in college the author worked at a buffet restaurant. The restaurant business is quite competitive. Those who do not know how to treat their customers often do not stay in business long. On one occasion a worker had a full pan of hot corn that she was going to place in a buffet island. A customer, not looking, backed into the worker causing her to drop the pan of hot corn. The hot water, butter and corn went flying all over the area including all over the customer's dress.

The customer was irate. The general manager quickly rushed over to the customer apologizing to her *even though he had seen it was her fault*. He gave her four tickets for free meals. Then he told her to have her dress dry-cleaned and bring in the receipt and he would reimburse her. Yet before she could respond he offered to buy her a new dress if she preferred! The author couldn't help but think that when this lady retold these things to her friends and family everyone would come to the restaurant hoping to have hot corn spilled on them.

Employees must be taught "A soft answer turneth away wrath: but grievous words stir up anger." Prob. 15:1. The attitude of the businessperson and his or her employees toward the customers ought to be: "How can we best serve you?" This is not only good business but also the example left to us by Christ. It is no coincidence that ServiceMaster was named such. It was started by a Christian to do business in a Christian manner. Paul makes service out to be a Christian duty. "For, brethren, ye have been called unto liberty; only use not liberty for an occasion to the flesh, but by love serve one another." Gal. 5:13.

Many in the workforce today do not understand economics so the managers in charge of them must teach them such. One poll indicated half of Americans thought the government had its own money. After seeing these results the author began asking some workers questions about where the government gets its money. Most thought the government got money by just printing it! If the government's money can't be followed back to the taxpayer, it is no small wonder that a company's money can't be followed back to the customer.

As mentioned in an earlier chapter, regardless what company we are working for, we are working for God. Laurie Beth Jones expounds on this theme. "Jesus did everything AUTL. As Unto the Lord. When he made a chair he wasn't making it for Joseph, really. He was making it for the Lord. If every single person in business could have and practice this philosophy, imagine what kind of customer service we would have in this country. One of the surest signs of spirituality in business is excellence." While this is not something a non-Christian employee would understand, it should be part of the Christian manager's example.

Most employees, including managers, have only self-interest at mind. While every disciple of Christ knows what havoc self-interest brings into daily living, it similarly causes many to neglect the interest of customers. Many employees are more concerned about getting themselves in trouble than they are about pleasing the customer. The auther once had a manager, in a grocery store, refuse to allow him to exchange a pepperoni pizza he had mistakenly purchased for the cheese pizza he wanted. The pizza cost only 99¢ and the receipt showed the purchase had been over $99. As she was defending her decision, he politely interrupted her. Only after reminding her that he purchased groceries there each week and that would change if they were not customer-orientated she changed her mind. How many other customers they lost due to following such silly policies only God knows.

Rules are established in business for the benefit of the company, employees, customers or a combination of these. Perhaps not as much today but years ago many gas station require all customers to prepay for gasoline before being allowed to pump it. There were exceptions to that for those that frequented a station often. In fact, one of the reasons some people would frequent a specific station was because they make such exceptions. The rule is established for the company, the employees and the customers. Prepaying makes the employees' job easier. He or she does not have to be so watchful of those pumping gas. Losses incurred by gas theft result in higher prices on the soda pop, potato chips and other items in the store. Thus a prepay policy benefits the customer. The policy benefits the company by reducing gas theft and making the operation of a gas station easier.

While the policy is good for everyone involved, exceptions can be made as part of customer service.

Some believe God makes exceptions to His law under certain circumstances. I disagree. If God were able to make exceptions to His law Jesus would not have had to die. Forgiveness could have been granted without the blood of Christ. However man has misunderstood the law of God to the point that it seems God has made exceptions to it. This is most clear in the gospels where Christ and His disciples were regarded as Sabbath breakers. The Pharisees said, "Behold, why do they do on the Sabbath day that which is not lawful." Jesus responded by repeating the story of how the priest, Ahimelech, gave David hallowed bread that was for the priests. While giving David the hallowed bread may have been against the letter of the law as found in Leviticus 24:5-9 it was not against the law's intent. Ahimelech did not casually give David the bread without regard to the ceremonial law. He required that David and his men be sanctified just as Israel was at Sinai (Exodus 19:14, 15). There was no exception made to the law's intent.

The exceptions made to business' polices in regard to customer service often do not violate the policies' intent either. Those who want to read a policy word by word and establish iron rules are often possessed with the same spirit as the Pharisees. The Pharisees believed that by adhering to a strict set of laws they could earn entrance to heaven. While these laws were based on the Scriptures, their interpretations were of men and much was added to them. Such interpretations did not lend themselves to making provisions under any circumstances. Ellen White in *The Desire Of Ages* wrote, "The Jewish leaders looked with heartless indifference on human suffering. In many cases their selfishness and oppression had caused the affliction that Christ relieved." "It is the love of self, the desire for an easier way than God has appointed that leads to the substitution of human theories and traditions for divine precepts. To His own disciples the warning words of Christ are spoken, 'Take heed and beware of the leaven of the Pharisees.'"

The spirit of the Pharisees can be seen in behavior of many employees toward customers. I have heard this referred to as the pharisetical attitude. It is not only the desire to follow a policy word by word regardless of its intent, but is often filled with hypocrisy. That is the belief of one set of rules for the customer and another set for the employee. The same employee that refuses a customer in-store credit for an item that was bought on sale insists he or she be allowed to exchange an item without a receipt. The airline employee that refuses to hold a plane a couple of minutes for a passenger that was sent to the wrong gate later insists on a discounted fare because of a canceled flight. Without daily surrendering ourselves to God we will always have a tendency to be self-seeking and hypocrites.

Mark Eppler tells the story of a bank that refused to validate a customer's parking because the customer didn't technically make a transaction. The customer was a millionaire and changed banks as a result. The bank lost hundreds, if not thousands, in interest because of employees wanting to follow a policy letter by letter. Such poor customer service still exists in our world today.

That is not to suggest that everything must be done to please an unreasonable customer. However some degree of effort still needs to be made to please even the unreasonable. In the construction industry the general contractor subcontracts various portions of the work to subcontractors. The general contractor is then the customer as far as the subcontractor is concerned. A subcontract agreement is made and the work begins. Often times the subcontractor is asked to do more than their scope of the work. The subcontractor must decide how much work outside of their scope they are willing to perform in order to service their customer. If they do none the general contractor will most likely not want to work with them in the future. If they do too much they may not only lose profits but incur unwanted liability.

During his early college days, the author worked in a gas station that had a car wash. Unfortunately it was often out of order. Car washes were to be free if a customer filled up with gas. When it was out of order they gave out tickets for a free car wash. On one occasion a customer became very vulgar when offered her ticket for a free car wash. There were several other customers in line behind her as she began to swear and cuss about the car wash never working when she came. The author spoke to her kindly, bearing in mind that I didn't want her to leave the store with a bitter taste in her mouth. Even the unreasonable need to be granted some measure of customer service.

As far as the Christian is concerned, God is not only the Owner but also the Customer. Christ told us, "Inasmuch as ye did it unto one of the least of these My brethren, ye have done it unto Me." Matt. 25:40. Not only are we instructed to treat everyone as if they were Christ but we are told some may actually be angels. "Let brotherly love continue. Be not forgetful to entertain strangers: for thereby some have entertained angels unawares." Hebrews 13:1, 2.

Each Christian manager must ask him or herself why they are doing what he or she is doing. If one is in the restaurant business is it not to serve wholesome, delicious food in a timely or elegant manner? Does one not produce products in the manufacturing industry for a specific purpose? Those in agriculture feed the world. Those in construction build homes, bridges and roads, factories, ships and airplanes for the betterment of society. Educators teach us mathematics, how to read and analyze information. Mechanics, repairmen, maids, medical workers, drycleaners, musicians, minors and tree trimmers all provide services our world requires. Once the Christian understands why he or she is in their profession they must do it with all their heart.

When we feel good about what we are doing we will be better prepared to take care of our customers. 1 Corinthians 10:31 tells us, "whatsoever ye do, do all to the glory of God." This is not limited to diet. I like how verse 33 reads in the Contemporary English Version. "I always try to please others instead of myself, in hope that many of them will be saved. You must follow my example as I follow the example of Christ." It is that type of selfless attitude that brings glory to God in all that we do and makes for fine customer service.

Poor customer service often results from the perception that the customer is an annoyance. It is not uncommon for a worker to speak harshly to a customer because of something the customer has done or said. Employees need to be instructed to refrain speaking harshly to customers under any circumstances. "Let no corrupt communication proceed out of your mouth." Eph. 4:29.

Words cannot be swept up and disposed of like a broken jar. Words are like dry leaves on a windy day. They are blown to and fro and no one really knows where they end up. If an employee speaks harshly to a customer that customer goes out and tells others about the incident. Those others tell still more. Like leaves blowing about, no one knows how many people have been turned away from the place of business due to the nasty tone expressed in only a few short seconds.

Teamwork

Teamwork plays an important part in customer service. Wal-Mart boasts of its great customer service and points out that they have no employees. Every worker in Wal-Mart is given stock options. They have many associates but no employees. Many do not understand what is involved in being a team member. Creating a working team is one of a manager's great challenges.

One of the reasons military experience looks so good on a resume is that members of the military are among the few in American society that know what it means to be a team player. Military units are trained to be mission orientated.

The author was once reprimanded for what would have been saving the life of a comrade. His unit was using MLS gear for training. This type of gear uses lasers to simulate real war conditions. Instruments are attached to rifles, anti-tank and anti-aircraft weapons. If a soldier is hit, his or her alarm will sound. Tanks have strobe lights that will go off and oil will be sprayed onto the manifold of a helicopter producing a cloud of smoke if hit. His squad had just ambushed another squad and we were pulling back. One of his comrades was left behind and yelled for suppressive fire to allow for him to escape. As the author went to do so his squad leader told him to forget it and pull back. He disregarded the order of his squad leader and placed himself in danger of being hit in order to provide suppressive fire. Both the trapped comrade and the author were able to escape but he was not a hero. He placed the welfare of one soldier above the mission. He was thinking of the individual instead of the group.

It took some time to be able to understand the reprimand and agree with it. It seemed awfully cold-hearted to leave a man to die because the mission was more important. However by placing more importance on a man's life than on the mission he jeopardized the mission. If wars are going to be won they must be won one mission at a time. The purpose of most wars supposedly justifies the loss of life. As a soldier one must commit him or herself to being a small part of something big. Being a team player is a requirement.

Teamwork is most visibly taught in drill and ceremony. Everyone dresses the same, marches in the same step and moves at the same time and in the same direction. When one individual makes a mistake, everyone is punished. This teaches those who are strong to teach those who are weak. No one stands out. Each individual is a small part of something big.

Blue collar and corporate America are filled with individualism. This is not a reference to rugged individualism that teaches one to strive to be the best they can be. It is a reference to what is known as chronic individualism where the individual looks out for him or herself first and last. Many workers today are more concerned about how their career is going to progress than about how successful their company is going to be. When the company starts to talk about decreasing pay for a short term due to financial problems, the employees begin to send out their resumes.

These self-centered individuals often lack patience with those who are in need of training and motivation. Rather than those who are experienced and talented in the trade "bringing up" the newer and less experienced, they favor replacing them with someone better. It isn't that there are not lazy workers that need to be terminated. Some are lazy and there are also those who are not smart enough to do a job requirement. Yet many workers have been fired because their manager and coworkers didn't want to put forth the effort to train and motive them. Most who speak of teamwork do not understand the concept. It requires a line of thought that is foreign to most.

While managers are to be team-orientated, we are allowed to be compassionate. Sometimes a Christian manager may choose not to lay off a worker knowing the hardship the worker would face. Such a decision may actually not be in the best interest of the team. Such decisions should be made after much prayer and Christian counsel. Not laying someone off for purely personal reasons should be the exception rather than the rule. Such decisions are rarely easy but it is much like having to leave a soldier behind. Often times companies shrink instead of grow and workers must be laid off.

Creating a team begins with the manager acting like a team player. Motivating employees to work toward company goals will also produce results. There are several ways this can be done. Many companies give employees shirts or jackets with their logo on them. Profit sharing programs contribute to a team environment as do company parties and newsletters. Creating a team is not going to happen with just one thing. It is a number of things. A team environment rarely will occur unless management makes it a goal. Each employee must understand that company goals are achieved because each employee does their part.

Some small-business owner's idea of team work is that the whole team works for him or her. There is a form of self-centeredness in which the owner of a company is totally focused on self to the point they become fearful of anyone taking advantage of them. What they considered being taken advantage of is constantly evolving. In their mind, they should be the only ones benefiting from the company. They will pay employees and give benefits only to the extent required to keep the company profitable and competitive. If they discover they are paying an employee more than a competitor, they start feeling that they are being taken advantage of – even if the employee is an instrumental part of producing the company's profits. They have a warped concept of what a team is. Yet, they will speak of building a team and the need for everyone to work as a team.

Part of customer service is creating a work environment that employees enjoy working in. A suggestion box can be helpful. This allows customers and employees to offer suggestions and criticisms. It is often times hard to accept criticism but the Christian manager needs to not only accept it but seek it. The psalmist understood this when he wrote, "Let the righteous smite me; it shall be a kindness: and let him reprove me; it shall be an excellent oil, which will not break my head" Ps 141:5.

Being a team member ought to be a humble experience. It means being a small part of something big. Much like our role in the plan of salvation. As individuals we have no major role to play in the plan of salvation. However collectively as the church, we have a large role to play in the plan of salvation. Therefore it is humbly that we serve each other as we serve God. We do not wish for those weak in the faith to be thrown off the team. Paul wrote, "Brethren, if a man be overtaken in a fault, ye which are spiritual, restore such an one in the spirit of meekness" Galatians 6:1. Rather those of us that are strong in the faith are instructed to strengthen those that are weak.

There are also times in the church we must make tough decisions. However difficult it is we must sometimes rebuke, censor or even disfellowship a member. This is done not only for the "team" but also just as importantly for the member. Christ told us, "As many as I love, I rebuke and chasten" Revelation 3:19. The church cannot be as effective of a tool for God if it allows open sin to be practiced without corrective action.

When our workers have the sense that they are part of a team they will work harder and produce better results. Even if they never see the customer, it has a significant impact on customer satisfaction. Those who have employees working with customers will be much quicker to realize the value of teamwork. A team member joyfully smiles and is helpful. The author once waited in a long line at Wal-Mart to make a purchase. As the cashier began to ring up his items he commented that she had a lot of customers behind him. She replied that at that moment she only had him. The implication was that she would do whatever was needed to see that he left satisfied. She was a team member.

Profit sharing plans work well for many firms. Waitresses are quick to learn the value of customer service. This is due to much of their wages being in the form of tips. A waitress quickly learns that the better service the customer receives the more profits she will earn. She also learns that the more she can get a customer to purchase the greater her 15% tip will be. By giving the waitresses a cut of the profits (in the form of tips), restaurant owners increase their own profits. The waiting staff works with the interests of the restaurant in mind. A typical profit sharing plan will cause the employees to realize that the better the company does the greater they will each individually profit. This will be discussed more in chapter seven.

The Public Trust

Customer service means working to serve the customer. What this means in some industries is not always clear. Who, for example, is the jailers' or policemen's customer? Who is the customer for the courthouse clerk or the state-licensing center? In many cases the taxpayers, as a whole, are the customer and not the individual being dealt with. That does not mean the individual should be neglected or abused unnecessarily. Just as those working in private industry, those working in the public trust ultimately are working for God. Individuals should be treated with respect when possible.

People seem to be viewed more as annoyances by those occupying bureaucratic positions than their peers in private industry. A bureaucrat has no competing business that threatens his or her job and is often a member of a labor union that provides job security. Unfortunately these facts tend to allow those in the public trust to treat the public however they may feel like treating them. This will not be the case for the Christian employee.

Government in America is viewed as a necessary evil. Government is not viewed as something that the people want but rather something they need. Police, prisons, road crews, public health workers, military personnel, firemen, judges, schoolteachers, etc. are all needed by society. These positions, like government, are made by the people and for the people. Therefore those who hold these positions of public trust are but trusted servants. A Christian will understand that and act accordingly.

Many occupying bureaucratic positions are less than friendly because those requiring their services often are not too friendly themselves. It is a vicious circle. The person requiring the service knows from past experience that at the local courthouse, licensing center, etc. there will be long lines and poor service. Therefore they arrive with a sour attitude. Those working are not motivated to provide good service because, it seems, all those they must attend have sour attitudes. If the vicious circle is to be broken those employed in the public trust must do it.

Distant Customers

In some industries the customers are rarely seen. Some factories manufacture parts for other factories. Many wholesalers supply retailers that they never see. Yet even these too have customers to consider. These customers demand products and services in specific quantities at specified times. In order to meet these deadlines each of a company's employees must be customer orientated from the assembly line worker to the delivery driver.

The consumer will not likely choose a factory or wholesaler that cannot deliver on time. However if deadlines are consistently met a customer will rarely give ear to one's competitor. Those working for these companies need to be made aware of whom the customers are. Meeting deadlines will meet customer expectations.

Employees should be reminded and commended when deadlines are met. Goals should be set and celebrated when achieved. Celebrating, commending and reminding keeps customer service in the minds of those who rarely see the customer.

There are companies known for their expertise in their field but that know very little about customer service. They have an attitude that since they were so skilled in their trade that they were doing their customers a favor. Some have been recognized within their industry for excellence. Their status in their respective industry can go to their head to the point where they think they are doing the customer a favor and not the other way around.

Most everyone is familiar with the words customer satisfaction. Yet few understand what it requires. Christian managers must do all that is possible to properly train employees to be customer orientated. Employees must understand that their paycheck comes from the revenue received from the customers. It is the customers that provide their livelihood. Therefore there is an unwritten debt to each of a company's patrons. A manager's example must never conflict the training given to employees. A manager should not complain about customers and expect employees to great them with a smile under all circumstances. Customer satisfaction is the fuel of a successful business.

6

Problem Solving

Scripture teaches us that we must look outside ourselves for answers. Paul wrote, "I can do all through Christ which strengtheneth me." And Christ clearly made the point, "without Me ye can do nothing" (Philippians 4:13; John 15:5). Christ Himself was an Example of this dependence. "The Son can do nothing of Himself, but what He seeth the Father do... The words I speak unto you I speak not of Myself, but the Father that dwelleth in Me, He doeth the works." (John 5:19; 14:10). With this knowledge, the humble manager learns how and where to look for solutions when problems arise.

A good manager is not one that knows everything rather one that knows where to find anything. Solving a problem often has more to do with finding the answer than having the answer. It requires identifying options and testing them. Proverbs 11:13 says, "in the multitude of counsellors there is safety." Problem solving frequently requires a manager to consult others. Those may range from others more experienced, subordinates, peers and perhaps attorneys.

There too are many problems that are solved before they ever come about due to prevention. It is said, an ounce of prevention is worth a pound of cure. That applies to business problems as much as it applies to medicine.

Counsel

It is a great mistake to think that one's point of view is always correct. Some go as far as surrounding themselves with others that adore them. The advice Ellen White once gave to a minister can find its application to businessmen and women too. "You must not walk independently of all counsel. It is your duty to counsel with your brethren. This may touch your pride, but humility of a mind taught by the Holy Spirit will listen to counsel, and banish all self confidence." *Testimonies To Ministers And Gospel Workers* p. 315.

Our vanity not only causes many problems that could have otherwise been avoided but too often prevents us from finding solutions for problems we find ourselves in. As a Christian we should not hesitate to seek criticism. A friend who is willing to criticize us is of much greater value than one that does not dare. Yet not all criticism comes from our friends. The criticism that comes from those who oppose us should not be dismissed only because of its source. Christian managers need to place a high value on all criticism. Constructive and well-intended criticism is always for our benefit. That criticism that is not so constructive or well-intended can teach us a lesson in patience and good manners.

To receive counsel from others, it is helpful have a network of others to consult. There are many ways to network. Becoming active in trade associations and attending seminars may be two of the most effective ways. One can also build a network of others be joining athletic clubs, community organizations, softball leagues, your children's PTA or even within your church family.

When seeking counsel from others one must do so in a prayerful and genuine manner. The danger of speaking to many consultants about any given situation is that one is bound to find another that agrees with his or her preconceived ideas. The purpose of seeking council is to find the best solution to a given problem. It is not to confirm that our own line of thinking is best. Often times the Christian manager seeks the morally right solution to a given situation. If those giving the advice are somehow connected to the situation we must be cautious as self-interest may influence their opinion.

Consider one of the author's experiences. During the construction of a building it was discovered that a subcontractor had omitted a portion of his work. The contract documents were not clear about what materials were to be used in this portion. One of the options was to consult with the subcontractor about what type of material should be presented to the architect for approval. Of course the advice the subcontractor would be influenced by his self-interest. The author first consulted one of the subcontractor's competitors. Then he spoke with an architect not connected with the project. After that he was in a position to speak to the subcontractor about it. He had a couple of third-party views and was in a better position to judge the opinion of the involved subcontractor.

In this example the author did not want to cheat the owner of the project by using inferior materials. However he didn't want to unfairly burden the involved subcontractor by forcing him to purchase materials that cost more than what could have been used. Since the subcontractor omitted the item, its cost was never in the price the owner agreed to. Therefore the owner was never charged. However since it was shown in the plans the subcontractor had an obligation to include it, even if he had omitted it by error.

Right and wrong are not always crystal clear. Let's say the above example involves a door. The building plans show a door so a door must be provided. Since no material is specified any of a variety of doors could be installed in its place. There are steel doors, wood doors, aluminum doors, solid doors, hollow doors, plastic doors and still other types. If one were to simply ask the project's architect he is likely to choose the most expensive and difficult type to install. The subcontractor is likely to choose the opposite. There is the dilemma.

We are not to look to spiritual advisors as having God-given authority. Spiritual advisors do not decide what is right and wrong for themselves or anyone else. What one should hope to find in a spiritual advisor is one that knows the Scriptures from both study and experience. Given one's circumstance they can often show them scripture that is helpful in deciding upon a solution. It is God, though His Word, and not the advisor that holds the authority.

Not all council applies to everyone equally. It is a mistake to think that there is only one solution to a given problem. The old adage says, there is more than one way to skin a cat. There are those who believe what is right for them is right for all. Commenting on the adage they would say, "There may be more than one way to skin a cat but none is better than mine." This kind of thinking limits solutions. The Christian manager needs to make room for the idea that he or she may be mistaken.

Pride really doesn't serve a manager well. Yet it pops its head up everywhere and at every chance it gets. Pride will sometimes prevent one from consulting the person with the right answer. Pride will cause one to criticize others that think differently then he. It is pride that fools one into believing his or her way is the best way. Such thinking leads to arrogance. A manager's arrogance often leads to low moral on the part of the workers, less efficiency and higher turnover.

Laurie Beth Jones in *Jesus, Inc.* wrote, "How do we integrate surrender into the business plan? I struggle with the question daily… We will get where we need to be only by admitting we do not know the way" (p 38). Our surrender to Christ includes laying at His feet our business problems. Running a business our way will not result in the glorification of God. The Christian manager must admit that he or she cannot solve problems as Christ would have them do, unless Christ is a part of each solution. Prayer is very powerful but godly council cannot be neglected. When one neglects to seek such council it is often because he or she does not admit the need.

Prevention

Laurie Beth Jones, in the same book, tells of a commercial she saw and what she learned from it.

> A television ad I saw recently made me laugh. It showed Noah and his wife checking off the animals as they entered the ark two by two. "Ostriches." "Check." "Peacocks." "Check." "Rhinoceros." "Check." "Termites." "Check." There is a pause as a look of horror crosses Noah's face. "Termites?!" he yells. "Call [XYZ] Pest Control!" In the final scene the [XYZ] truck is shown being driven onto the ark. No wonder Noah survived the flood. He didn't let little problems grow into big ones. p. 189

Many problems creep up on us and can be prevented or taken care of while they are still minor. Often times counsel given in their regard is ignored. Consider for a moment a neglectful employee that compromises safety regulations. On a few occasions comments are made to the boss that the worker should be terminated as he is going to get hurt and perhaps cause others to get hurt as well. Or there is a machine that is showing signs of failure and comments are made about it needing to be replaced. How should one respond when the boss calls looking for a mechanic to fix the broken machine at two o'clock in the morning or that his workman's compensation insurance is expensive due to preventable accidents?

Choosing the right worker for the job can prevent a lot of problems. Proverbs 26:10 reads, "Like an archer who wounds everyone, So is he who hires a fool or who hires those who pass by." Wrong workers are hired for a variety of reasons. Sometimes the labor market does not have the skilled workers that are required. In such cases a company needs a training program. Sometimes the company doesn't want to pay the wage required by skilled workers. That may be solved by training and if not a higher wage may need to be paid. Sometimes poor workers are hired simply due to carelessness and for that there is no excuse.

Wrong employees can turn away many customers that would have been satisfied. They can cause good employees to quit and seek other employment. They can increase deficiencies in products. They can cause more products to be returned for warrantee work. Money saved in wages for a cheap worker too often is spent or lost due to their performance.

It has been said that no training can make up for hiring the wrong person. This is another reason it does us well to understand personality types. Placing the wrong person to do a task often creates a problem that was preventable. Supervisors should be trained to observe personality conflicts among workers and report them to their superior so such matters can be monitored. Where training fails discipline must be utilized.

Insurance and Sureties Problems

Some Christians believe that purchasing insurance shows lack of faith in the protection of God. I do not want to take the time in this book to address this issue. The law requires many types of insurance and even business people who would otherwise not purchase such policies must deal with problems involving them.

Many times business problems involve insurance and sureties companies. Insurance is something everyone wants to have but no one wants to use. The insurance or sureties representatives are to ride in a white horse with a big checkbook. Managers often get frustrated when it seems the representatives are coming in on the back of a turtle. Frustrations can be unfairly taken out on the representatives.

Christian managers need to remember that regardless what the problem is the insurance or surety company was not the cause. The insurance and sureties companies cannot be faulted for looking out for their own interests. That is not to say they are justified in unduly denying claims. However with the epidemic of fraud that they must deal with daily, it would be foolish for them not to double check everything, dot all their i's and cross all their t's.

The first rule in dealing with these representatives is to be friendly. Remember they have the checkbook. Even though they are contractually obligated to you, they are experts in their industry. If there is a way for them to get out of their obligations or lessen them, they know what it is. No manager wants to give any insurance or surety's representative reason to take such action.

I do not want to suggest one be all smiles and laughs to the extent that he or she will be perceived as a chump that can be taken advantage of. One should pray before meeting with the representative. Everything should be in order so any documentation that is requested can be quickly and easily provided. Organization shows that a manager is no chump to be dealt with. It also makes the representative's job easier and thus any payout quicker. This is ultimately what a manager's goal should be in dealing with the situation.

Sometimes it becomes necessary to get a lawyer involved. In some companies, it is simply standard practice for a company lawyer to be involved with all insurance claims. Caution should be used in this area and counsel is a must. If a lawyer is brought in, he or she is going to take a significant portion of whatever the settlement ends up being. Many in the legal profession have a competitive spirit. Once two lawyers (or teams of lawyers) start battling, you can be sure the insurance or surety company will be looking for ways to get out of obligations or lessen them.

While no manager wants to be shorted on a claim, each needs to use desecration in settling it. Working out a claim is no time to get greedy. The Christian manager should be willing to compromise in areas that legitimately deserve it. What one needs is to receive that which is required by the policy or contract between one's company and the insurance or surety company.

These companies market themselves as being there to help with problems. The Christian manager needs to work with them in such a way that allows them to do exactly that. Faith, patience and good manners will go a long way in achieving that end.

Having Our Lives in Order

A manager whose life is in order is going to be more successful at analyzing situations, seeking counsel and solving problems. This may not seem like the area of the book that this theme would be discussed but it is directly related to the success of a businessperson's ability to diagnose and attack problems that arise.

Our lives cannot be so easily divided into areas like the spiritual, business, family, social, etc. Problems one has in one area of life are often times going to affect other areas. If one has difficulties controlling one's temper at work he or she may think it a business problem when it may well be a family or social problem. One who is struggling with financial problems at home may become distracted more easily in the office. Our spiritual life affects our family, business, social, financial and church life. These other areas of life also affect one another.

Jesus gave the greatest advice in the Sermon on the Mount. Many have been literally singing it for years. "Seek ye first the kingdom of God and His righteousness, and all these things shall be added until you." The Christian manager needs to keep the spiritual house in order. Time needs to be spent in study and prayer. There are few of us that spend as much time in prayer as is needed. Worldly distractions need to be eliminated such as inappropriate television, movies and sporting events. Our time away from the office should be valued as much as our time in the office. Time is a limited resource of which none of us really knows how much we have.

Jerry Bridges in his book, *The Pursuit Of Holiness*, states something that should be obvious to every Christian but bears repeating. "We need a planned time each day for reading or studying the Bible. Every Christian who makes progress in holiness is a person who has disciplined his life so that he spends regular time in the Bible. There simply is no other way. Satan will always battle us at this point. He will try to persuade us that we are too sleepy in the morning, too busy during the day, and too tired at night. It seems there is never a suitable time for the Word of God. This means we must discipline ourselves to provide this time in our daily schedules."

The Christian Manager cannot place too much value on the spiritual life. Christ has promised that if it is placed first than all the other things will be added. When a problem arises if one's spiritual life is not in order he or she will often become panicked, angry, frightened or some other state that will disrupt clear thought processes. "The fear of the Lord is the beginning of knowledge" Prov. 1:7 and Christian managers need knowledge especially when trying to solve problems.

Too many have allowed themselves to become complacent in their spiritual lives. After first accepting Christ most are energetic in Bible study and attendance of prayer meeting. The spiritual life of the new believer is often the most important thing to him or her. However Satan works on each of us to cause us to leave our first Love for things of the world. It is a great error to put off the things of God to pursuit business. We are directed to pursuit first the kingdom of God and His righteousness and all the other things will be added unto us. That is a promise of God. God is faithful to keep His promises. He is not forgetful that we have reason to doubt Him. We are asked to try Him – to put Him to the test. If we are to maintain balance and order in our lives we must not distrust the voice of God.

Analyzing Options

Once a Christian manager is faced with a problem and has consulted others for solutions, he or she must analyze the options. Most every problem has various possible solutions. We may gather various options from our consultants and some of them may even help us analyze them. However often times our consultants are not so much spiritually minded as they are industry minded. The world is not filled with born-again Christians, so it is that Christians must deal with non-Christians, and often seek their advice, regularly.

Time does not always allow a manager to consult with a spiritual advisor about every problem after speaking with industry-minded consultants. It would be ideal if that were the case but often time decisions need to be made quickly and being able to consult someone who is industry minded is a luxury. Then too are those calls that must be made without consulting anyone. So how is a Christian manager to make the right decision?

Scripture gives us the promise of being transformed to be like the Lord (2 Cor. 3:18). This comes about as we study and practice the Word of God. There is an adage that says, "Show me a man's friends and I'll show you the man." We are influenced greatly by the people we choose to spend time with. This is no less true with Jesus. The more time we spend with Him in prayer and study of His Word, the more He enables us to begin to think like Him.

While the Lord does tell us in Scripture, "My thoughts are not your thoughts" it also commands us, "Have this mind in you, that was also in Christ Jesus." Isa. 55:8; Phip. 2:5. On our own our thoughts are not as God would have them be. Yet we are invited to have the mind of Christ. The more time we spend with Christ the more we will be influenced by Him and begin to see things as He does.

No where does Scripture instruct us to rely on human opinion as a basis for our decisions. However Proverbs 27:17 tells us, "As iron sharpens iron, so one person sharpens another". Human feedback can enlighten us in regard to technical and personnel knowledge. Our network of consultants can offer advice about personnel and industry-based problems due to their expertise and experience. The Christian manager must find the answer for spiritual dilemmas in the Word of God. When we spend enough time in God's Word and studying it with dedicated believers, our thinking does change and we see God's answers more easily than before.

Thus it behooves each Christian manager to spend time in meditation with scripture. There is no other way for anyone to have the mind of Christ. Managers make decisions all the time that affect people's lives. The manger's relationship with God will have a direct bearing on how problems and solutions are analyzed.

The time to assign blame for a problem is after a solution has been decided upon. Placing blame often takes effort away from analyzing before a problem has been solved. There will always be time to place blame after the problem is solved. The parties to blame for a problem are sometimes the same that hold the solution. Blaming and disciplining them before a problem is solved can cripple productive efforts. The Christian manager needs to be level headed about such things.

7

Profits

Not all organizations are profit driven. However most companies and corporations are. Profits are the lifeblood of most businesses. Without sufficient profits a business will not be able to continue. Some Christians struggle with the question of how much profit is needed. The marketplace should determine that. In an open marketplace competition should always make sure one doesn't profit too much. Most industries have a code of ethics that can serve as a loose guide to the Christian manager. The word loose is used because a Christian's ethics will often be higher than that established by a given industry.

In a column published by the Jewish World Review on June 26, 2002, Walter Williams defines profits as a price. "Profits are the prices paid as residual claims to entrepreneurs in their role as risk-takers, innovators and decision-makers." Profits are not an evil thing that should be kept to a minimum. Companies profiting are good for society because they increase the value of resources. An example is silica sand. Silica sand was worthless until companies started to use it to produce a profit. The greater profit they could produce from their products the greater the value of the sand became. Examples of these kinds would be endless.

Larry Burkett in his book, *Business By The Book*, lists profiting, along with funding the gospel, meeting family and employee's needs and making disciples as the functions of a business. He points out, "Profits are the economic rewards of good service and products (normally)." The profits earned by Christian managers are not intended for selfish use. God provides these profits in trust. The Christian manager will be judged on how he or she uses what God has provided. God requires more than just tithing. Tithing is giving back to God what He never intended us to keep. The tithe belongs to Him and is not ours to use. Thus, many Christian managers dedicate 10% of their profits to be donated to charity or the church they belong to.

Profits should not be made at the expense of a company's employees. Employees should be paid a fair wage for the industry. Many companies offer profit sharing and stock option plans to employees as incentives. While much of a company's success is due to good management, it simply cannot be done without the common workers. A wise carpenter values and cares for his hammer. Without the hammer he would be unable to drive a single nail. His success depends on his hammer and so he cares for it. How much more should a Christian manager care for his/her employees than does the carpenter for his hammer?

The time each of us has on this Earth is limited. However, the amount of money we can make is not limited in the same respect. Our lives will come to an end and the trust God granted to us will be passed on to someone else. Scripture tells us God "hath appointed a day, in which He will judge the world." and "God shall bring every work into judgment, with every secret thing, whether it be good or whether it be evil." Acts 17:31; Eccl. 12:14. Each of us will have to give an account of how we spent the profits God afforded us.

Marketing

Marketing is required by most businesses as a means of getting knowledge of their products and services to their perspective clients. Some businesses need to market their goods and services more than do others. However many businesses have failed due to poor marketing. Some mistakenly believe they cannot afford to market their products and services and in reality they cannot afford to neglect it. The Christian manager will not only be concerned about marketing but also about the means employed.

Much of marketing today is sex. Sex is not only used to sell clothing and perfumes but cars, shampoo, gasoline, soda, and the list goes on. While Christians believe the sexual instinct is God given and pure, it is wrong to promote sexual behavior that is outside of God's will in order to increase our businesses. Profits derived from the promotion of sin do not come with the blessings of God. While they may provide temporary success it is shortsighted and unfaithful to embrace them. Scripture points to the example of Moses saying, "By faith, when he was come to years, refused to be called the son of Pharaoh's daughter; choosing rather to suffer affliction with the people of God, than enjoy the pleasures of sin for a season." Hebrews 11:24, 25.

Sin can bring temporal pleasure (and profits) but brings with it pain and eternal consequences. Those who use sex to promote business may never know how many hearts were broken because their marketing campaign encouraged sinful sex. How many children grew up without fathers? How many diseases were passed around? How many teens ended it all after sexual romances went bad? Those who have purposed in their heart, as did Daniel, to remain loyal to the Lord of heaven, will not make a sexual appeal to increase profits.

Dishonesty is often embraced in marketing. Claims are made for products and services that are not true. Competitors are often slandered. Such are not methods a Christian manager would want to embrace. If one cannot honestly market his/her product or service then s/he needs to get out of the business and find what God has in store for them.

80/20 Principle

The 80/20 Principle is also known as the Paretho law. An Italian economist named Vilfredo Pareto in 1897 discovered the principle. He observed that 80% of the world's wealth was held by 20% of the population. Richard Koch has written a book called simply *The 80/20 Principle* where he provides the history of this and thought provoking examples of its use.

It is a principle of disproportionalality. That is to say that most things are disproportionate like 80/20. Eighty percent of ones problems with employees result from only twenty percent of the employees. While it is rarely 80/20 it seems that it is often closer to 80/20 than 50/50. By taking note of this a manager's attention can be targeted to the 20% rather than the 80%. Too often 80% of the employees may suffer due to the 20% that are causing problems. A fair manager can use this principle to avoid making such mistakes.

Other examples are as follows: 80% of profits come from 20% of a firm's products. 80% of crime is committed by 20% of the population. 20% of the clients purchase 80% of the products or services. 20% of the mistakes result in 80% of the complaints. 20% of the employees earn 80% of the payroll.

It is showing the disproportional relationship two sets of data have to contrast each other. Let's look at the problems Christ encountered as one set of data and draw a relationship between it and the population of His area. It was 20% (or a small percentage) that caused 80% (or a large percentage) of His problems. This is unlike the story of Elijah during the reign of King Ahab. 80% of Elijah's blessings were the result of 20% of the population.

This principle has its application to both our professional and spiritual lives. The attitude one has 80% of the time may have a relationship to the way one spends 20% of the time. One may spend eight to ten hours each day at work yet the three to six hours spent each day with the family produce a good attitude for 80% of the day. The reverse may also be true. The daily family life may result in producing a bad attitude most of the day. Discovering what produces results will allow one to improve those results.

As businessmen and women we want to increase profits and stability for our company. This principle would teach us that 20% of our efforts produce 80% of our profits. So what should one do with the 80% of the efforts that produce 20% of the profits? These tasks can be delegated to a less paid, less skilled employee or eliminated altogether. The idea is to make the most money by spending the least amount required doing it.

The 80/20 principle can be used to identify where a company's profits are coming from by dividing the company into groups. There are several ways to divide them including its customers, products and geographic regions. In commercial construction owners would be government, private industry and individual investment. Products would include schools, office buildings, retail buildings, roads, bridges, utility, factory, medical facilities, telecommunications, aviation and shipping facilities. Geographic areas would include the company's hometown area, state, bordering states, nation and international areas. Once categorizing a company's profits, the 80/20 principle will often show that the profits are disproportional and a company strategy can be made to reflect it.

One area may show to be very profitable however very little of that type of product is sold. In the construction example we may look at utility and factory work. Utility work may make up 20% of a company's profits, while only making up for 5% of the company's work. Factory construction, on the other hand, may make up for 50% of the company's work but only be producing 35% of the profits. These groups can be rated by the amount of profit they produce, the company's share in them and their attractiveness. While factory construction may not produce high profits, the ease of construction makes it an attractive market and the company has a large share of it locally.

Complexity

The old adage, "Keep It Simple Stupid" has its application in business. Business complexity almost always leads to waste. Thus it is known as the cost of complexity. The simpler a business can be, the more efficient. That is not to say we shouldn't pursuit volume. However we shouldn't blindly pursuit it. Many businesses are so complex that the right hand doesn't know what the left hand is doing. This leads to many things having to be done over again.

A large telecommunications company once employed a firm to build a project for them. While the company earned several hundred million annually their complexity cost them much of it. One example is of a door opening that they decided to close up. This cost them nearly an additional five thousand dollars because it was not in the original plans. A few weeks after closing it they decided they would need the opening after all and paid just over five thousand dollars to put it back. So it cost them ten thousand dollars because one group didn't know what another was doing.

There are many other examples. Mistakes are made that cost a company money. Rather than establishing a standard operating procedure (SOP) so as to avoid the same mistake, other employees continue to do the same. SOPs reduce complexity. They result in everyone doing the same task the same way. A popular restaurant chain put signs in the kitchen that read "Do Not Memorize Recipes". The company wanted all the cooks preparing the food in the exact same way.

SOPs will vary in detail depending on the task. Different people work differently. An SOP's purpose is not to make everyone work exactly the same. It is to prevent errors that have happened or are foreseeable. The attitude that everyone must do everything exactly the same often discourages creativity and morale. The object should simply be to prevent errors and inefficiency.

Project Management

A project manager's job description is not always easy to define. A project manager does not do any one task rather he or she runs projects. This often involves working with several people or groups of people. In construction a project manager deals with architects, owners, subcontractors, vendors and employees. In advertising a project manger works with clients, draftsmen, actors, spokesmen, media salesmen, etc. It is a job that can become very complex very quickly.

To maximize profits the project manager needs to try to take the complex and make it simple. Listing the main goal of each project can start this. Then milestones can be made for each project. Completing the project becomes like connecting the dots: each milestone is connected in order, ending with the project's goal. Possible problems may be anticipated along with possible solutions.

It becomes almost like running a circus. There are several groups of people with varying tasks at varying stages. Often times some will not complete their tasks on time or even show up when scheduled. A manager can become very stressed at his/her lack of control over a situation. The Christian manager will need to remember that God is in control. It is His guidance that is needed.

A manager cannot control anyone. He or she can encourage, advise, motive, entice and threaten people. However their reaction to the manager's tactics is beyond the manager's control. Acknowledging this truth eliminates a lot of stress from a manager's job. Jesus does not control us. He invites us to take His yoke but never forces us to take it. The idea that we must control our fellowman can become an obsession until we are no longer able to enjoy life.

Project managers have to work with what they have. Different areas of the country (or world) are going to have different labor forces or perhaps even tools. Some areas are better educated while others may be more dedicated. The project manager needs to know what s/he is working with. Once that is known options can be made as problems arise. It becomes business rather than an emotional, stressing knot. Evaluate the options, pray, seek godly counsel if needed and make the decision.

Sharing the Profits

A profit-sharing plan is a great way to motive employees to production and excellent service. Unfortunately some employees are seemingly unable to be motivated. Increasing their wages, benefits and giving them bonuses doesn't seem to produce much change in their work efforts. However many employees will become more dedicated and become more productive and profitable. Thus by sharing the profits with the employees, the profits increase.

The principle of disproportionalality tells us that a small percentage of the employees will produce a large percentage of the profits. In light of this it reasons that this group of employees should receive the largest bonuses. Some companies have only a small group of employees that receive profit-sharing bonuses. In such cases that group should be made up of those producing the large percentage of profits. Bonuses reward behavior. If we award someone who produces little, it is presumptuous to assume they will start producing more.

Due to the complexity of organizations it is not always easy to identify exactly how much each employee has produced for the company. Let's look at a couple of examples. A car dealership makes money from new cars, used cars, parts and service. A young salesman that has only been with the firm a few years may be selling economy cars, which produce marginal profits for the firm. A much older salesman who has been employed for the firm many years sells luxury cars that produce significant profit for the firm. The young salesman is the better salesman and the only reason he produces fewer profits is because he has been limited to economy car sales. Not only is that an injustice to him but mismanagement on the part of the dealership. Normally his bonus should be based on the profits he generated for the firm. However if he is not compensated for his ability he is likely to find another employer willing to do so.

In the same dealership there is a manager in parts that often does paperwork for the service manager. He does this because time allows him to and the service manager is much busier. Since he is not only running the parts department but also helping with the service department, his profit-sharing bonus ought not to be based only on the profits generated by the parts department. When he understands that part of his bonus comes from profits made by the service department his commitment to teamwork is likely to increase.

The larger the company is the greater these problems of evaluating how much specific employees produce for the company become. Often times one must rely on accounting data which results can depend upon the method of accounting used. If considerable thought is not given, employees producing less will be retained and those producing more will look for other employment. Thus we find yet another cost to complexity.

Too often managers allow personalities to influence the size of bonuses given. Some may receive sizable bonuses because they are very popular in the company. While others producing twice as many profits receive a bonus of the same size. Should the one producing more profits find out he or she is not only like to become unmotivated but likely to start looking for another employer.

Salaries and Benefits

Salaries and benefits come before profits and therefore are not part of them. Salaries should be fair. The marketplace and competitors determine this. What does the market allow a company to pay its employees? What are its competitors paying their employees? If there is a union involved it plays a role in both the market and competition. It is erring to think that paying an employee a salary is sharing the profits with them. Profits are a company's earnings after all the costs are paid. Those include the cost of labor.

Benefits are determined much by the market, competitors and the employees often play a role. Years ago a small firm offered all its employees a choice of adding health insurance as a benefit or taking an increase in salary. It was a small firm but all employees had to vote. The choice was health insurance for all or a raise for all. The employees chose health insurance.

To determine what is fair pay for an employee one need only look around at what their competitors are paying. Sometimes this varies a lot. A conversation with a local job placement agency or a state unemployment office can often provide information about what the prevailing wages are for specific positions. Companies normally get what they pay for. Companies that do not pay well typically will either have a high turnover or have employees that are not as educated and experienced as others and thus produce more defective work.

Compensating an employee isn't just about salary. Employees are going to want benefits like other companies provide. These benefits include such things as vacation and insurance but can also include company parties, use of company vehicles, cell phone, computers, private office space, etc. According to the US Bureau of Labor Statistics (BLS) the average private company provides hourly workers seven paid holidays and salaried workers receive an average of eight and a half. That can be contrast with an average of eleven paid holidays provided to the average public-sector employee. 89% of private companies claim to provide paid holidays and 90% offer paid vacations. BLS also reports that the amount of sick days increases with the amount of time an employee is with the company.

So how does a company pay for these benefits? The employee earns them. The company charges the cost of the employee's wage to the product or service being sold. Consider a salaried worker earning $1,000/week. The base salary is $1,000. To that is added the labor burden. The burden includes the cost of insurance, matching Social Security and paid time off. If the employee has eight and a half paid holidays, ten vacation days and five sick days that is a total of twenty three and a half days or 188 hours. At $25/hour ($1,000/week) that is a cost of $4,700. There are 2,080 working hours in a year. Subtracting the 188 from that, there are 1,892 hours remaining. The $4,700 is divided by the 1,892 to get $2.48. Thus for each hour the employee works, the company needs to charge an additional $2.48 to pay for the paid-time-off. The company must also match the Social Security, Medicare and pay worker's compensation. For the sake of our example, let's say the company also pays $400 per month for health insurance. The labor burdon would then be as follows:

Paid time off	$2.48
Social Security	$1.55
Medicare	$0.36
Worker's Comp	$0.88 (rate varies depending on various factors)
Unemployment	$1.25
Health Insurance	$2.50
Total Burden	$9.02

So in this example the base salary is $25/hour and the burden is $9.02. Thus the cost of the employee is $34.02/hour. That cost has to be included in the calculation for any goods and services an employee is producing. The cost is passed on to the end user purchasing the goods and services. The company than acts as a trustee. In theory, the company is collecting money from the customer and using that money to pay the employees. The profit is the amount above and beyond the cost of production that charged to the goods and services.

Jeremiah 22:13 and James 5:4 are two verses often used for paying one's employees fair wages. Many Christian managers would like to pay their employees top dollar and every benefit imaginable. However that would put many out of business in which case its employees would be looking for work elsewhere. Yet some managers underpay their employees simply due to greed. There is a middle ground. If a company is fair with its employees most of them will be satisfied and their efforts will reflect such.

In the author's hometown a manufacturing firm employed about 5,000 employees. Union representatives had been coming around and the employees were about to vote on becoming unionized. The company published a financial report in a newsletter for its employees to see. It showed the gross revenues, various costs such as labor costs, raw material cost, management cost and profits. It compared these to one of its competitors. After reviewing the newsletter the employees rejected the union.

Some employers always thank the employees when they hand them their paychecks. They well understand what the Lord meant when He said, "The laborer is worthy of his hire" (Luke 10:7). Employees provide needed service for companies. Without those services the companies could not profit. When they are compensated for their time and effort, it is a fair compensation. There is really no need for thanks from either the employer or employee. However a grateful employer will, of course, offer thanks as will the employee.

Salaried Workers

A salaried worker is someone who is hired to do a job and not hired by the hour. The employee agrees to work however many hours is needed to accomplish the job. If the job is supervision than the salaried employee's hours will be about the same as the workers he or she is supervising. Many believe the salary is based on a 40-hour week. The US Department of Labor (DOL) has not established such a rule. The salary is really task orientated. The DOL has established that thirty five hours is considered full time. Thus, as a general rule, salaried employees should be expected to work between 35-45 hours per week. However ultimately the salary is based on a task the employee is performing.

If the employee needs to consistently work over 45 hours a week in order to complete the tasks assigned to him or her, they probably need assistance. That would mean hiring an additional worker to help them with their duties. Of course, if the salaried employee can't keep up with the workload due to laziness, he or she may need to be replaced. There are managers that put in over 50 hours each week on a regular basis while other managers with the same workload are getting things done in 40 hours. Upon investigation, those putting in a lot of hours are actually chatting with vendors and workers and generally have a lot of unproductive time while those getting things done in 40 hours are managing time wisely and staying on top of tasks. So before an assistant is hired for a manager putting in a lot of hours, the work habits of the manager should be evaluated for productivity.

It is reasonable to expect a salaried worker to put in a lot of additional hours for a temporary period of time. A deadline may require a salaried worker to work up to 60 hours a week for a few weeks. In some industries there is a busy time of the year when salaried workers are required to work longer days. Many employers like to give these managers a little extra bonus but it should not be something that is expected simply because extra hours are required for a few weeks.

The Top Salary

The salary of a company's CEO and top management is often determined by how well the company is doing. Yet the compensation should be sensible. President George W. Bush, in his address on corporate responsibility, said, "I challenge every CEO in America to describe in the company's annual report – prominently, and in plain English – details of his or her compensation package, including salary and bonus and benefits. And the CEO, in that report, should also

71

explain why his or her compensation package is in the best interest of the company he serves."

Some company owners give themselves a low salary and cash out on bonuses. Basically they draw a salary from the company and every quarter will give themselves a bonus based on the quarter's profitability. This helps prevent them from living on the feast-or-famine rollercoaster.

The pursuit of profits can lead to dishonest business practices that do not resemble the character of our humble Savior. God does and has blessed many men and women with the temporal wealth of this world – honestly earned. Yet that wealth is but a trust and its rightful Owner is He who granted it. "For we brought nothing into this world, and it is certain we can carry nothing out. And having food and raiment let us be therewith content. But they that will be rich fall into temptation and a snare, and into many foolish and hurtful lusts, which drown men in destruction and perdition. For the love of money is the root of all evil: which while some coveted after, they have erred from the faith, and pierced themselves through with many sorrows. But thou, O man of God, flee these things; and follow after righteousness, godliness, faith, love, patience, meekness. Fight the good fight of faith, lay hold on eternal life, whereunto thou art also called, and hast professed a good profession before many witnesses. " 1 Tim. 6:7-12

The author's royalties from this book go to fund Christian education.

www.ingramcontent.com/pod-product-compliance
Lightning Source LLC
Chambersburg PA
CBHW021441170526
45164CB00001B/336